shell life & shell collecting

By Sonia Bennett Murray

Photographs by Gilbert L. Murray, Jr.

STAR SHELL

AVENEL BOOKS · NEW YORK

ACKNOWLEDGMENTS

This book is dedicated to Gil Murray, my husband, who not only suggested I write it, but whose patience, encouragement, and assistance helped bring about its completion. I owe a debt of gratitude to Dr. Harald A. Rehder of the Smithsonian Institution for his time and efforts, and to the United States Air Force who placed at my disposal the Air University Library at Maxwell Air Force Base, Alabama. I also want to acknowledge the expert advice provided by Veronica Johns in checking the manuscript and pictures. The picture on page 80 is reproduced by courtesy of the British Museum and the one on page 83 is from the "Guinness Book of World Records".

In addition, I owe thanks to the many friends and relatives who offered advice and provided me with specimens from far countries. Helena Clarke, my grandmother, deserves a special mention as the person who first introduced me to the wonderful world of shells.

517119234
Copyright © MCMXIX by Sterling Publishing Co., Inc.
Library Of Congress Catalog Card Number: 70-90799
All rights reserved.
This edition is published by Avenel Books
a division of Crown Publishers, Inc.
by arrangement with Sterling Publishing Co., Inc.
a b c d e f g h

HEART COCKLE
Corculum cardissa—3"
Indo-Pacific region.

Contents

1. Introducing Shells and Shell Dwellers 5
    The Five Classes of Mollusks 7
    How Classes of Shells Evolved 15
2. How Mollusks Live 21
    Nurseries of the Sea 21
    How Shells Are Made 25
    The Battle to Live 29
3. Collecting Mollusks 41
    Finding Perfect Specimens 41
    Cleaning and Displaying Shells 66

Shells in Color 49

4. Man and Mollusk 73
    Shells in Prehistory 73
    Shells of the South Seas 82
5. Mollusks as a Business 87
    Food for a Hungry World 87
    Jewels from the Sea 89

Index 94

FURBELOW CLAM
Tridacna squamosa—4"
This beautiful "frilled" Clam is from Siasi in the Sulu Archipelago in the Philippines. Found on coral reefs, its frills camouflage its outline against the coral. All Giant Clams have this general structure.

FLORIDA HORN SHELL or FLORIDA CERITH
Cerithium floridanum—1"
Lives in shallow water. Eats detritus and is a useful scavenger. The abundant Horn Shells are a valuable food source for waterfowl and fish.

1 Introducing Shells and Shell Dwellers

DID YOU EVER HOLD a seashell to your ear to listen to the "roaring of the waves," or pause on a beach to look at gaily colored shell dwellers left stranded by the falling tide? It is hard to resist these bright souvenirs, strewn free for the taking at the water's edge in a glistening profusion of shapes and colors. Most tourists take a pocketful home with them. Although the little animals that make shells, called mollusks, live almost everywhere, on land or sea, shell collecting is a hobby that usually begins with a visit to the coast.

It may be that you already have a few shells, and would like to know more about them. They are doubly interesting when you know how they were made and how their owners lived. Also, in order to build up a collection of perfect, shining specimens you must know where and how to look for them. Many beaches are littered with shells, but most of them have been bleached by the sun and broken by the pounding of the surf. They look pretty when wet, but as they dry their sheen and color disappear. Every year, like amateur prospectors bringing home fool's gold because they do not know what to look for, tourists by the thousands gather the beachworn shells and take them home, only to throw them out in disappointment when their colors fade.

Take a look at the shells you may have collected: most of them are probably beachworn, but one or two may be shiny and new looking. If you found these a short time ago they may still contain the remains of their mollusk-builders. These "freshly dead" shells are better than the beachworn specimens, but usually they are not so perfect as the shells you find alive. To find live shells you must know where they live. You must also know how to clean them and remove their occupants, or your budding collection will smell abominable and end up in the dump heap.

Those who start collecting shells rarely stop. "Shelling" is a hobby that gives its devotees great pleasure at nominal cost. We may live in a complex, sophisticated city, but many of us never lose our fascination for the sea. We find it relaxing to potter about the rocks and marshes and sandy bays that mark the ocean's meeting with the land, to hunt for shells, to watch the little creatures in the tidepools. Some collectors find their hobby leads them on to serious study; many of the scientists who work with mollusks grew interested in them after picking up a few for souvenirs during a childhood vacation.

People are not always interested in shells because they have succumbed to the collecting urge. Mollusks are interesting in themselves. It is absorbing to watch a garden snail laboriously inching its way up a blade of grass or making Herculean efforts to climb over a twig in its path. The study of shells that lived millions of years ago helps geologists to determine the age of rocks, and paleontologists to learn how living things evolved. Some of these ancient species of shells are found in rock which may contain oil deposits, so oilmen who would not know a snail from an oyster are jubilant when they find a shell.

Mollusks have a long and fascinating history intertwined with a greater history, the story of mankind. Shells took a part in human life before our remote ancestors left their caves, serving as food, utensils, and ornaments. Later on, their use as money and objects of barter stimulated trade and helped to shape the patterns of civilization. The story of man and mollusk deserves to be more widely known.

Although scientists have learned a great deal about shell dwellers there are still gaps in our knowledge. Very little is known about the shell population of some remote parts of the earth. Even in civilized regions new varieties are still being discovered. Shells come in a wide range of shapes and sizes, and no one knows exactly how many different kinds, or species, there are. Educated guesses range between 70,000 and 100,000 species.

It would be impossible to describe each of these species in detail in a single book, or to do more than skim the surface of the great body of knowledge about them that has been compiled over the centuries. Tomes have been written about the shells of North America alone. This book, therefore, is intended only as a beginner's identification guide with advice of primary interest to shell collectors. It is a book about shells—what they look like, how they are made, and how they live—and about the ways in which men have used them from prehistoric times to the present day.

Luckily for us, scientists have simplified the task of identifying and learning about shells by grouping similar kinds, or species, together into families, and families with similar characteristics into classes. Let us start by seeing how this was done, and what the members of each class look like.

The Five Classes of Mollusks

Long ago, when scientists began to classify everything on this planet, they found that each living thing or object was either an animal, a vegetable, or a mineral. They named these three great groups "kingdoms." The animal kingdom, the one that concerns us here, was found to contain creatures with backbones and creatures without backbones—vertebrates and invertebrates. Then these subdivisions were broken down into races (phyla) of similar animals. One such race of invertebrates, the phylum Mollusca, contains the animals which make shells.

Mollusk merely means soft-bodied. Like many other words you will meet in shell study, it is derived from Latin. There was a time when every educated man could read and write Latin fluently, and when no scholar would think of writing in his native tongue. Latin, therefore, was the language of science. Today the students of dead languages are few. But Latin terms live on, because they serve as an international language for scientists and collectors all over the world.

Marine mollusks are sometimes grouped according to the depth of water in which they live: those from the ocean floor are "abyssal," those living on or near the shore are "littoral," and those which swim or float in the surface waters are "pelagic." This broad grouping of thousands of mollusks has obvious deficiencies, so they are divided in another and more useful way. All mollusks possess an organ called the FOOT, which has evolved into five radically different forms. All the species which have the same kind of foot are grouped together into a class. The foot is only one of several anatomical differences which set the members of the five classes apart from each other. Their external appearance is distinctive, too. It seems strange to think of anatomy in connection with such shapeless blobs as oysters and slugs, but even these humble creatures possess senses, nerves, a digestive system, and a heart. The study of molluscan anatomy, in fact, is a science in itself!

The largest and most important of the five classes contains the Snails, Slugs, and Conchs (pronounced "conks"). These mollusks, and all the others in this class, each possess a large foot, located directly below the head, on which they crawl or glide. This unusual form of transportation gives the class its name, GASTROPODA, meaning "belly-footed." A Gastropod moves along in a series of ripples; it extends the tip of its foot, presses it down against the ground for an anchor, and contracts it to pull the rest of its body forward. It has eyes mounted on two fleshy stalks, which children call horns, at the tip of its foot, where its head is located. Most Gastropods make shells that circle around an AXIS or COLUMELLA, spiralling to the right. These right-handed species are called DEXTRAL.

A typical Gastropod.

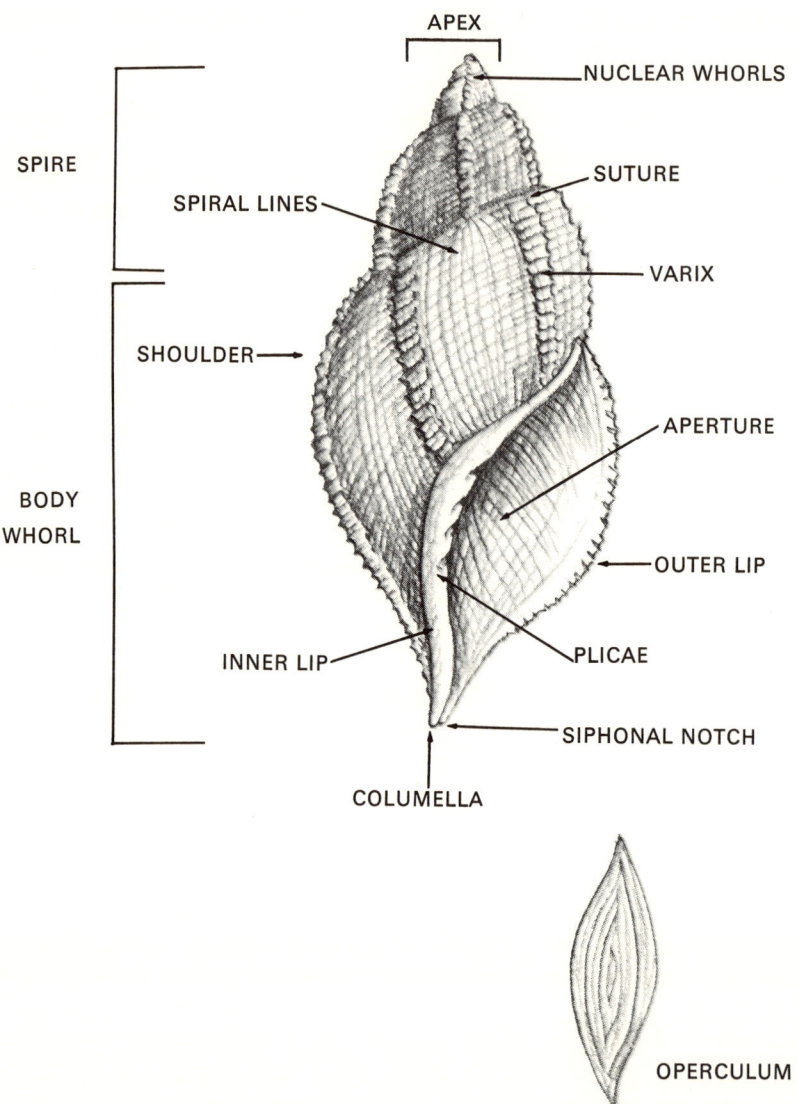

Occasionally species which make dextral shells form a shell which spirals to the left instead; some Gastropods always make left-spiralling or SINISTRAL shells. All Gastropods make their shells in one piece, and for this reason they are often called UNIVALVES, meaning they have one valve only.

Take a look at a Conch shell. The first complete revolution, at the apex or tip, is called the NUCLEAR WHORL; it was the original shell of the baby mollusk, later added to and extended to fit its growing owner. The revolution at the bottom of the shell is the last made, or BODY WHORL. The nuclear whorl and all others except the body whorl form the SPIRE of the shell. At the end of the body whorl you will see an opening, through which the body of the living mollusk protruded. This opening is called the APERTURE, and its edge the LIP of the shell. Some species have a horny trapdoor, the OPERCULUM, attached to the tip of the foot, which is the last part of the body to be withdrawn when the mollusk retreats into its shell. When the foot is pulled in, the trapdoor closes the aperture tightly, as raising the drawbridge seals a castle doorway. The operculum is also used as a claw to pull its owner along.

Gastropods vary greatly in size, from tiny species too small to be seen with the naked eye to Giant Conchs 2 feet or more in length. The heavy shells of these larger species afford excellent protection, but like any other form of armor plate they are heavy and awkward to carry around. Some Univalves, such as Slugs, have lost their castles and learned to rely on darkness to hide them from their enemies, staying under leaves or stones in daylight and coming out to feed at night; others, for example Sea Slugs and Sea Hares, depend on speed and smoke-screens rather than fortresses to keep them alive.

The Land Slugs and Sea Hares have not lost their shells completely, although the only remnants are internal and completely useless. The Land Slugs, as every gardener knows, are unpleasant looking creatures that seem to take a perverse pleasure in feasting on the choicest young vegetables and half-opened flowers. Sea Hares live on seaweed and are chiefly notable for the violet-pink liquid which they emit when molested. This liquid is a protective device, serving as a screen to confuse their enemies while they escape. The Sea Hare has a pair of tentacles projecting from its head which give it a slight resemblance—if you have a good imagination—to a crouching hare.

Sea Slugs or Nudibranchs (the name means "naked or exposed gills") are often very beautiful, having gaily colored mantles which undulate as they move through the water. The MANTLE is a vivid, delicate envelope of flesh enclosing a mollusk's soft inner parts, comparable to our skin. In many species the GILLS, which are equivalent to the lungs of higher animals, have disappeared, being replaced with capillary veins close to the surface of their bodies which extract oxygen from the water. Other species have gills, carrying them in feathery rosettes on their backs; these exposed gills give the group its name. Nudibranchs eat sea anemones and seem to be immune to their poisonous darts; in fact, they are said to assimilate these darts into their own bodies and release them as weapons against their enemies!

The Sea Butterflies or Pteropods, another sub-order of the Gastropods, are small free-swimming creatures that have traded the foot for fins. The Pteropods lose their calcareous shells soon after they hatch, and replace them with the delicate snow-white winglike structures that give them their name. (Pteropod means "wing-footed.") These little creatures are found floating on the ocean in vast swarms, and are so abundant they form a staple food of whales.

Now let us take a look at the second great class of mollusks. This class, PELECYPODA, contains such common species as clams and oysters, which make two-piece or BIVALVE shells. The word Pelecypod means "hatchet-foot," and as one might expect, many Pelecypods do have a hatchet-shaped foot. In this class the foot is used to burrow and dig in mud and sand, rather than for crawling. Pick up an empty Clam shell and look at it. You will see that the VALVES were held together in three ways: by interlocking ridges or TEETH around the margins, by similar teeth at the apex (between the two prominent humps, or UMBONES), and by the powerful pull of the Clam's ADDUCTOR muscle or muscles which have left a scar where they were attached to the inside of the valves. An elastic cartilage called the HINGE joins the valves together between the umbones, but this cartilage tends to pull the valves apart. When the Clam wants to open its valves it does so by relaxing its muscles and letting the powerful spring of the hinge pull its shell open.

The Clam's valves are known as right and left; it is fairly easy to tell which is which, since the umbones usually point to the front and the twin breathing tubes, called SIPHONS, toward the rear of the shell. Look at the inside of a valve: scars marring its smooth finish tell a great deal about the anatomy of the animal that lived there, and are often described in handbooks as a means of distinguishing between similar species. There are large scars where the adductor muscles were attached to the shell; the MANTLE or PALLIAL LINE connecting these scars shows where the tissue of the mantle rested. The PALLIAL SINUS, a v-shaped dent in this line dipping toward the margin of the shell, marks the place where the bulky siphons protruded between the folds of the mantle. Collectors call a bivalve shell with its valves still joined at the hinge a PAIR.

Bivalves are lower down on the scale of life than Univalves; they have little or no head, and usually lack eyes. With the exception of a few free-swimming species, they are sedentary (stationary), finding a permanent homesite early in

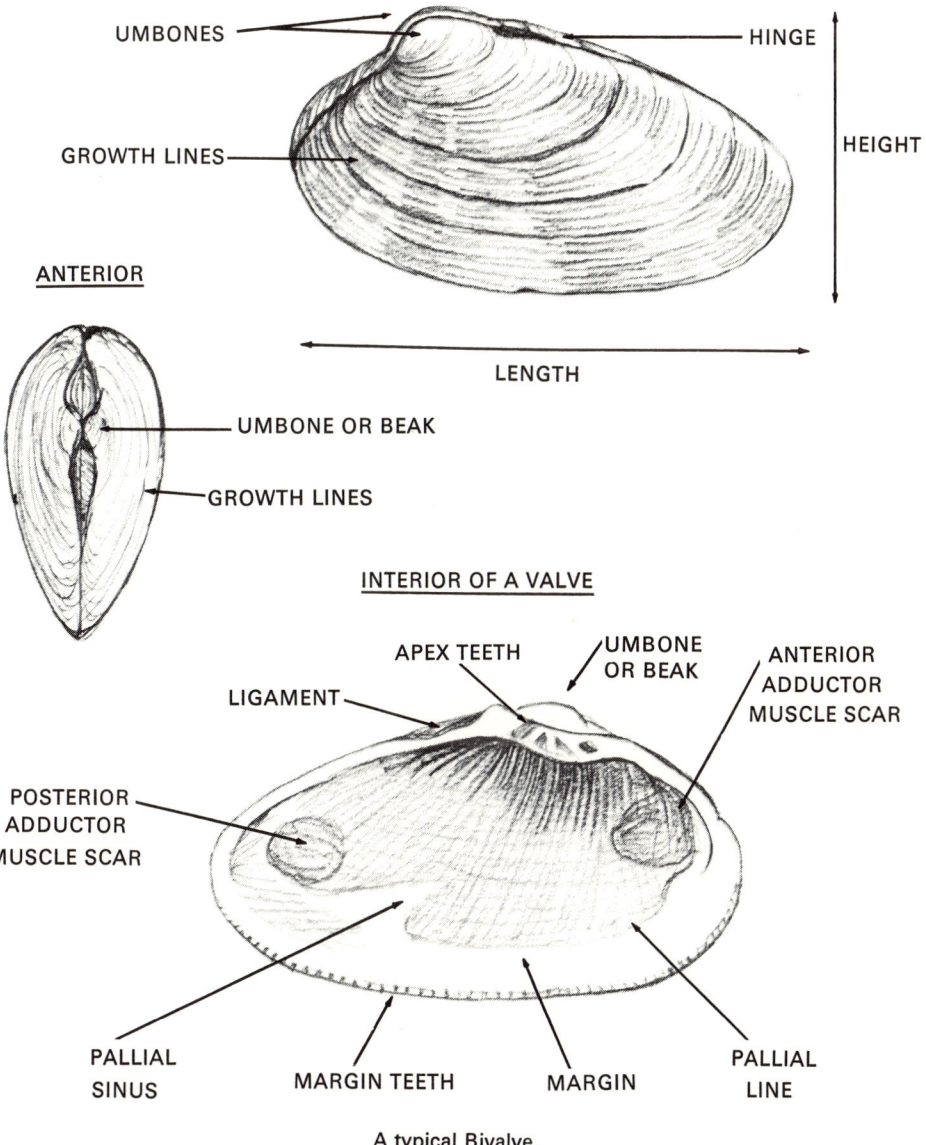

A typical Bivalve.

11

life and settling down to a peaceful existence. Their sedentary way of life probably accounts for the fact that Pelecypods grow larger than Gastropods; a shell that is thick and heavy is good protection for a mollusk that spends its life in one place, but it would be a fatal handicap to an animal that had to move about quickly in search of food. There are a few microscopic species, but most of the Bivalves reach a fair size and some of them are massive, the largest species being a 5-foot Giant Clam found in the South Seas. The valves of this monster often weigh 400 or 500 pounds, and are often used to form ornamental basins for outdoor fountains or lights.

The small class SCAPHOPODA make strange little shells that look like the tusks of carved ivory elephants. Because of this similarity the Scaphopods are often called Tusk shells, or Elephant Tooth shells. They are more closely related to the Univalves and Bivalves than to the other mollusks, for they have the one-piece shell structure of the former and the bilaterally symmetric body of the latter. Tusk shells are not often found; some collectors think them rare. Actually they are present around American coastlines in considerable numbers, but the North American varieties are all white or translucent, small, and very fragile. Most of them get shattered to fragments before being cast up on the beach, while those that survive are hard to see among the heaps of larger and more colorful specimens. As is true with the other classes of mollusks, the most beautiful Scaphopods are found in tropical waters. One tropical species, for example, grows to be 6 inches long and constructs a shell of delicate, beautifully sculptured jade green. The Gastropods can be found on land as well as in fresh and salt water; the Bivalves stick to salt water, though they can live in rivers; but the Scaphopods are more choosy and are only found in salt water.

The Chitons, which make up the class AMPHINEURA, have shells formed by eight overlapping plates joined together by a muscular girdle. This plate-and-girdle armor, which gives the Chitons their popular name of Coat-of-Mail shells, is ideally suited to their way of life because it allows them to expand and contract their protective coating along with their bodies to fit snugly against the irregular surfaces of the rocks on which they live. If you have visited a rocky shore you have probably noticed these little animals or found detached segments of their shells washed up on the beach.

The foot of the Chiton has been modified in still another way: it serves as a suction disc as well as a creeping organ. When it is frightened it clamps down with this suction disc so firmly that it can only be pried loose with a knife. If you forcibly remove the Chiton it will curl up into a ball, expanding its armor to the fullest extent and completely protecting its soft underparts. Although the foot and body, which are normally hidden, are often gaily colored, the armor is always

BROWN PAPER ARGONAUT
Argonauta hians—3″
A member of the Class Cephalopoda, the Paper Argonaut makes this elaborate shell as a cradle for its eggs.

SPIRULA (top)
Spirula spirula—1½″
This tiny squid lives from 600 feet to 3000 feet below the surface. Upon death, its body disintegrates and its shell rises to the surface.

TEXAS TUSK SHELL (below)
Dentalium texasianum—to 1½″
Mud or low tidal dweller, but some species are abyssal. Anchored by its protruding foot, the mollusk draws water down to it through its shell, the narrow end of which rises above the mud.

13

of a dull shade that blends into the colors of its habitat. Most of the Chitons are quite small, the largest species being about 10 inches long.

The fifth and last important class of mollusks, CEPHALOPODA, contains the Octopus and Squid. Octopi have played the villain in so many tall tales that their bag-like bodies, writhing tentacles, and staring eyes are familiar to almost everyone. Although these animals have no external shell and are very different in appearance from their relatives the Snails and Clams, they are true mollusks: at some time in the remote past their ancestors made coiled or conical shells as much as 15 feet long, and even now some species carry a vestigial remnant of shell within their bodies. The tough skin of the Cephalopod—the name means "head-footed"—is equivalent to the delicate mantle tissue of other mollusks. The head and foot are close together in Cephalopods, and the edge of the foot has evolved into a number of sucker-covered tentacles, which now ring the animal's mouth. As the name Octopus suggests, this creature has eight tentacles; Squids are decapods, having the eight tentacles plus two more extremely long, flexible arms. Squid and Octopi have similar saclike bodies, but the Squid is longer and more cylindrical in shape than his cousin.

While Octopi prefer fairly shallow water, the Squids are deep sea creatures and often grow to great size; records of specimens 50 feet or more in length are not uncommon. It is very probable that the sea serpents reported by mariners in the days of small sailing vessels were actually the tentacles of dead or dying Squid which had floated to the surface.

Recent studies of Octopi negate the old belief in their malevolence. They do not, it seems, make a habit of lurking in wait for swimmers and dragging their victims to a watery death. Scientists say that Octopi are timid creatures and retreat hurriedly when they see a large object like a swimmer. Authorities believe the deaths of many swimmers who have encountered Octopi were probably due to sheer panic. Whether the Octopus is or is not timid, the reputation it has acquired is greatly to its advantage, for most people leave even baby Octopi strictly alone.

The Octopus is perfectly adapted to its environment. It can swim rapidly, forcing water through its siphon with enough propulsive power to move it 2 or 3 yards at a time, and moving its tentacles as a swimmer uses his legs. For slower movement on the bottom it can walk, though rather clumsily, on the tips of its arms. It is the highest of all the invertebrate animals, having a brain comparable to that of a fish, and eyes equipped with a retina and cornea much like our own.

There are three other Cephalopods which are of interest to shell collectors: the Paper Argonaut, the Nautilus, and the Spirula. The first of these, the Paper Argonaut, makes a fragile, finely sculptured white shell as a cradle for its eggs, discarding the shell after the eggs hatch out. The collector who finds this shell on a beach has a treasure indeed. The Nautilus carries its tentacles sheathed within an oddly developed foot and shelters its body in the end of a flat coil of pearly material. As it grows too big for its old home it seals off the vacated space with a thin partition called a septa, and builds larger walls for itself. The Spirula makes a similar home, but its shell is small, white, and partially hidden within its body. The Cuttlefish is a Cephalopod, but it is of commercial interest only: it makes a flat, internal, limey plate which is hung in bird cages to provide the birds with lime. Its ink is sepia, the pigment used by artists.

As you can see, the basis for grouping these animals together is their body plan rather than their appearance. Various organs have been developed or lost in the members of the five classes we have discussed, making them very different in appearance from each other, but they all have basic similarities such as the foot and shell which distinguish them from members of any other class, and even greater differences which set them apart from members of other phyla. By now you are probably wondering how these similarities and differences came about.

How Classes of Shells Evolved

There are very few places on earth where mollusks do not dwell: both arctic and tropic zones, both mountains and deserts, both rocky shores and sandy bays have a population of highly specialized shell dwellers that cannot survive in any other environment. Yet these creatures, so diverse in appearance and habitat that few people realize they are kin, have all evolved from jelly-like blobs that somehow acquired the ability to take the mineral content of their food and convert it into a hard outer covering.

When these first shells were made, perhaps 600,000,000 years ago, the land masses of the world today were partially covered by shallow seas. Then, and for 2,000,000 years to come, the North American continent was largely under water. Mollusks found ideal conditions in the vast expanses of shallow water, and flourished and multiplied. As generation after generation lived and died, their empty shells drifted down to the sea bed.

Centuries passed away and the land, still unstable, folded and buckled and rose; the waters receded, leaving their ooze high and dry to be slowly covered by layers of dust. Reptiles were suited to the new conditions, and flourished in their turn; for 100,000,000 years their footprints and bones were left in the mud above the shells of the long dead mollusks. At last the land settled once more, the sea swept in, and marine debris entombed the reptile bones. In some places land and sea succeeded each other again and again as the contours of the land changed, until at last the seas retreated to their present level and the continents which we know today took shape.

The dust and debris of a day weighs little, but over the centuries tons were deposited. Beneath this weight the lower layers were compressed, hardening at last into solid rock. Minerals carried by seeping water replaced the shells and bones, gradually turning them to stone. Hardened mud preserved an indelible record of footprints and leaves.

All these petrified and preserved traces of bygone life are known as fossils. Like many of our words, the term "fossil" comes from Latin; originally it meant "that which is dug up." Fossils are of interest here because great numbers of seashells were preserved in this way. From studies of these ancient shells, and from experiments with living animals and plants, scientists have traced the evolution of mollusks from their simple beginnings in the primeval seas to their present complexity and diversity of form.

The oldest fossil mollusks that have been found to date look something like our modern Snails. Among the fossilized shells of the descendants of these first Snails, however, there are slightly different species. These new varieties resulted from a genetic change, or mutation, which occurred in their parents. Perhaps the first mutants varied ever so slightly from the parental coloring. If the new shade matched their surroundings more perfectly than the old it acted as camouflage, helping them to evade their enemies; if on the other hand it made them more easily seen, it probably brought them an early death. The mutants best adapted to survive in their world were the ones that lived to reproduce their kind. Since mutants breed true, the descendants of the surviving mutants also had the new color.

Although these first mutants were only slightly different from previous generations of mollusks, further mutations kept appearing, so that species became more and more unlike each other as well as their ancestors, as time went by. Closely related species evolved distinctive features that were different from those evolved by other groups; classes, and families within classes, appeared. Within 50,000,000 years three of our present-day classes had taken their places on the stage of life—the Gastropods, the Pelecypods, and the Cephalopods. The radically different mollusks, the Scaphopods and Amphineura, were not established on the scene until 70,000,000 or 80,000,000 years later.

Mutation and natural selection of the mutants best adapted to survive have done much more than produce different species: these processes have enabled mollusks to climb out of the sea and conquer a whole new world, the world of the land. Early mollusks were sea creatures, taking their oxygen from the water through primitive gills in order to breathe. Then a few Gastropods adapted to life at the margins of the sea, the rocks and shallow bays. These areas, rich in food and otherwise well suited to shell life, are not always under water. Rocks far down the shore are uncovered for a few minutes at low tide, while those high on the beach only know the sea during winter storms.

The rocks of the seashore proved to be a bridge to the land. Snails living there had to find a way of breathing during periods of exposure. One can only wonder how many Snails lived there briefly, only to die during far-ebbing tides, for how many thousands of years, or hundreds of thousands of years, before one mutant Snail that could take oxygen from the air through slightly modified gills came along. That it happened we know. Many adapted in another way, learning to creep into tidepools or survive buried under wet seaweed; today these species still exist, having found a satisfactory mode of existence without completing the transition from gills to lungs which their kin accomplished so long ago. The descendants of that first mutant air-breather went on to the land; after countless generations they lost the ability to breathe by extracting oxygen from water, and became true Land Snails. Place a Garden Snail in water and it drowns.

Every part of the body has been modified to allow mollusks to colonize different habitats. The ancestral foot is still a foot in Snails and Clams, but in Chitons and a few Bivalves it is now a suction disc, and in Octopi and Squids, tentacles. The mantle has been modified into siphons to enable Clams to live buried in mud. The Octopus has a beak of hard, horny material for breaking open crab shells; the Limpet has a toothed ribbon, or radula, for scraping algae from rock. Even within family groups, shells are of slightly different construction and composition, giving the most suitable combination of strength and weight and shape for the way of life of each species.

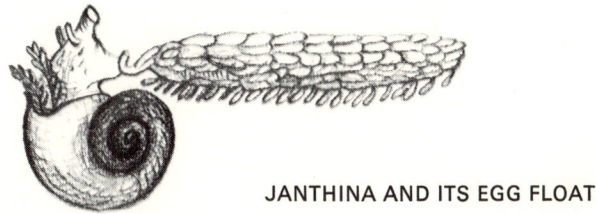

JANTHINA AND ITS EGG FLOAT

Many of our present-day mollusks have become so highly specialized, so beautifully adapted to the lives they live, that they can survive in no other environment. The Janthinas, floating Sea Snails with exquisitely beautiful lavender shells, are a perfect illustration of the advantages and dangers of over-specialization. Their shells, paper thin, are shaded from deep indigo at the apex to pale lavender-white at the base. The shell is attached upside-down, to a buoyant raft which the Janthina makes by trapping air bubbles in mucus. The raft keeps its

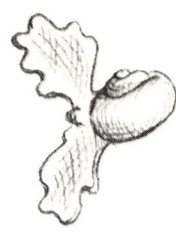 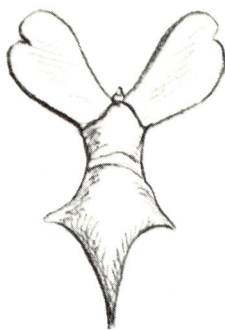

The Sea Butterflies have a coiled snail-type shell which they lose soon after they hatch and replace with winglike fins.

LISTER'S KEYHOLE LIMPET
Diodora listeri—1"
This Limpet lives on rocks around the low-tide level. It draws water in around the base of the shell, passes it over its gills and then expels it, along with wastes, through the "keyhole."

owner at the surface of the water and also serves as a cradle for its eggs. Winds and currents float the raft to the tiny jellyfish which the Janthinas eat. The raft and the coloring of the shell serve as camouflage, for birds see only the indigo base of the shell along with the raft and mistake it for sea foam, which they cannot eat. Fish peering up from below are equally confused, for they see the paler lavender of the apex against the white raft in the reflection and ceaseless movement of the surface waters and mistake the tasty shellfish for an unpalatable jellyfish.

Perfectly fitted for pelagic life as the Janthinas are, they cannot survive contact with the land. Each year storms bear thousands of the fragile voyagers into the shallows and dash their frail shells on the rocks or leave them stranded on the beaches. Even if their delicate bodies escape destruction on the impact with the shore the Sea Snails are doomed, for they are unable to creep back to the water; their long dependence on the currents of the ocean has resulted in their losing the ability to move around under their own power.

Even among more plebeian shell dwellers, the shape and strength of the shell has a lot to do with its owner's life expectancy. The Mussels, which live crowded together in colonies, on pilings and rocks exposed to heavy surf, prefer to ride with the storm instead of opposing it. They anchor themselves with threads of byssus, a tough, elastic material which can absorb the shock and pull of the breakers. Their shells are not heavy, but long and wedge shaped, streamlined so that the water glides harmlessly by instead of pounding and shattering. The Limpet has a different form of insurance against winter storms: it relies on a thick conical shell like a coolie's hat, and in the suction of its powerful foot to keep it from being washed from the rock. Its suction disc is strong enough to prevent a man from pulling the Limpet off, though it can be knocked loose if caught unawares, before it can anchor itself securely. Once anchored it can only be pried loose with a knife. Mollusks that live on sandy bottoms often have ridged shells which act as anchors, preventing the animals from being rolled about by the currents. These ridges may also help to keep the Drilling Conchs from getting the secure hold on a shell which they need in order to bore into it.

Mollusks that spend their lives in one place protect themselves with shells colored to blend into their surroundings. Octopi and Squid, however, are fast swimmers, pursuing their prey from the bright surface waters to the gloom below. Since their environment is not constant they must be able to vary their coloring as they move from place to place. It is doubtful that the steps through which this supreme camouflage system evolved will ever be traced, since the evidence would be found in cellular structure and in the heart of cells rather than in bones and other durable remains; but it must have been a sequence of small miracles. The Cephalopod's body is covered with cells, and each of these cells, or chromatophores as they are called, contains pigment. Some cells contain one color, some another; muscular walls can be opened or closed at the creature's will, enabling it to hide or reveal whatever colors it desires. How does the animal, with its limited brain, know when to switch colors and how to do it? With all its chromatophores closed it becomes jellylike and translucent, almost invisible in the water.

Everything man learns about the world around him teaches him more clearly the extent of his ignorance. There is much we do not know about mollusks, and much that probably can never be discovered. This we have learned, however: mollusks have evolved in diverse ways. They have adapted themselves in every possible manner, reshaping their bodies, shells, coloring, and life processes to enable them to survive in new conditions. They have evolved from simple Sea Snails to complex, highly specialized creatures colonizing every part of the world. They have reached their present level because, throughout the millennia, mutation has produced new species and natural selection has weeded out the unfit.

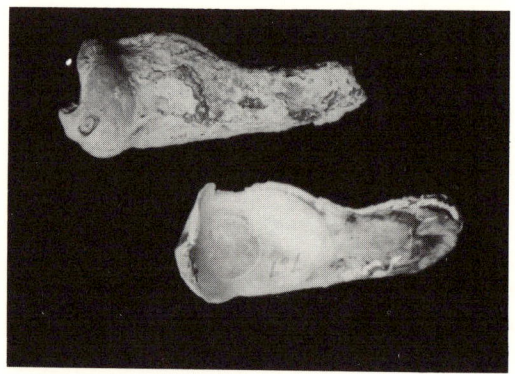

LISTER'S TREE OYSTER
Isognomon radiatus—2½"
This Tree Oyster clings to rocks and mangrove roots and can be easily found at low tide. Its brownish-yellow color serves as excellent camouflage.

2 How Mollusks Live

Nurseries of the Sea

THE WORLD OF MOLLUSKS is a world of teeming fertility and ever-present death, in which the chances of any individual egg surviving to reach maturity are small indeed. Vast numbers of Bivalve and Chiton eggs are never even fertilized, for the adult mollusks release their eggs and milt directly into the water and depend upon chance and the currents to bring them together. Long before the eggs which are fertilized reach the hatching stage they may be scooped into the hungry maw of a fish, or devoured by a sibling. Those that live to hatch out enter a savage, highly competitive struggle for existence in which only the luckiest and fittest survive. Exactly what the odds against them are no one knows; but authorities estimate that a female Oyster produces perhaps 300,000,000 eggs in a season, and the world is not yet overrun with Oysters!

The Conchs and Clams leave their eggs not as miniature Conchs and Clams as one might expect, but as top-shaped little larvae called "trochophores." Just as the embryos of higher animals and man take the shape of a fish in the course of their development, many invertebrates go through a trochophore stage before acquiring parental characteristics. The trochophores are free-swimming creatures with a built-in set of oars, a band of whip-like projections around their middles. These tiny whips or cilia beat against the water, moving them about and carrying them to the smaller forms of life which they eat. Later these cilia develop into lobes, and a visceral hump and a foot appear.

In this second stage of life the larvae are called "veligers." Trochophores and veligers alike live close to the surface, among the swarms of tiny creatures that make up the plankton, the staple food supply of the sea.

Life in the plankton is hazardous. Countless numbers of tiny fish browse upon these ocean pastures, while whales and other larger creatures swallow whole meadows at a gulp. The veligers that survive this carnage develop shells and take on their parents' appearance as they grow larger, and finally drift down to the ocean bed.

Here chance alone dictates the life or death of the young mollusks, for those

EGG CASES

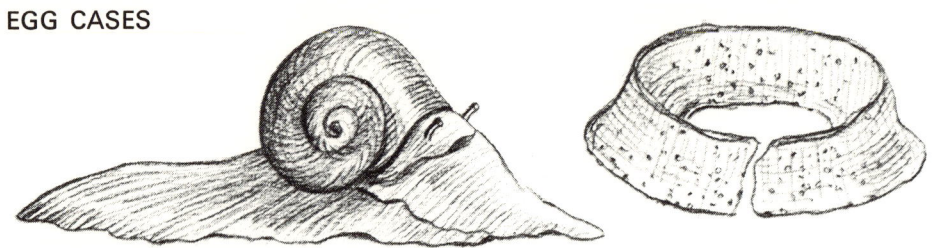

ATLANTIC MOON SNAIL
Polinices duplicatus—3"
The Moon Snail extrudes its eggs embedded in a gelatinous ribbon which hardens when it meets the water. The egg mass is shaped by the foot and base of the shell. The flared base of the "collar" lodges firmly in the sand, anchoring it. As it hardens, sand sticks to it and acts as a camouflage.

LIGHTNING WHELK

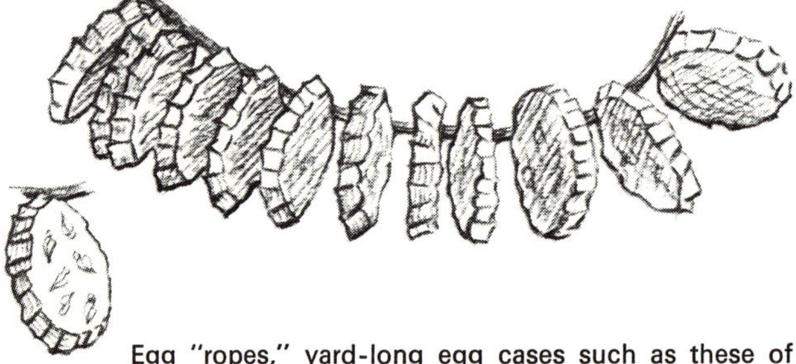

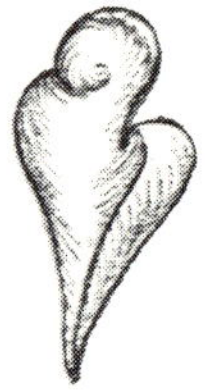

YOUNG WHELK

½"—1" Egg "ropes," yard-long egg cases such as these of the Lightning Whelk (page 58), are common on European and American shores.

PURPLE

Shaped like tiny bottles, the egg cases of the Purple, or Dog Winkle, are found in rock crevices. Each little capsule holds from 20 to 40 baby Purples.

BUCCINUM WHELK

These egg cases served as sailors' "scrub balls" in olden times.

that do not happen to settle in a suitable habitat are doomed. Many species have highly specialized needs—certain Snails must land on rock covered with adult seaweed or they will starve; Clams must reach a sand or mud bottom; and so on. Of the numbers that survive their defenseless weeks in the plankton, only a few will be lucky enough to reach the environment they must have to stay alive.

However wasteful this dependence on the sea's cradling arms may be, it has one great advantage: it ensures the widespread distribution of species that lead stay-at-home adult lives. The currents carry larvae far afield, to every habitat they can possibly colonize.

In more advanced species of mollusks the incredible wastage is reduced by increasing parental care of the young. Bivalves that rely on chance to fertilize their eggs must release great quantities of spawn into the water. Species such as Oysters improve on this to some extent, by keeping the eggs in the females' bodies until they hatch, fertilizing them with milt released into the sea by the males and drawn down through the females' siphons. When the young hatch, they are released to begin their life in the plankton. The vast quantities of eggs which these species produce make it evident that this limited care of the young, though better than nothing, is still most wasteful, as it does nothing to avert the great mortality occurring during the larval stages in the plankton, and in settling to the bottom.

A further advance is made by Snails that lay their eggs in protective egg cases. In some species the young are released as trochophores, in some as veligers; and in a few the eggs hatch and the young grow through the larval stages and develop shells before emerging from their case.

Egg cases are sometimes washed up on the beach before the young Snails break free; those made by Whelks are common on many shores. They are beige or brown, balls of pea-sized capsules or flattened, button-like discs joined by a band at one side into lengths that look like pieces of dirty rope. It is said that long ago, when soap was a luxury only the rich could afford, sailors used to scrub themselves with the sandy balls.

Other common egg cases are collar-like, sandy rings which you may have noticed in shallow water. These are made by Moon Snails; they lay their eggs in a ring of sticky material that gathers sand from the water as it dries, and so camouflages itself. Although protective casings cut infant mortality drastically they do not ensure the survival of every egg laid, for the young mollusks serve as food for each other until only a few of the strongest are left to break free of their walls.

In rocky areas, shell hunters often come across what looks like a bunch of black grapes, firmly attached to a stone near the low water mark. These

(Above) HAWK-WING CONCH. *Strombus raninus*—to 4". (Below left) LACINIATED CONCH. *Strombus sinuatus*—4". (Below right) ARTHRITIC SPIDER CONCH. *Lambis arthritica*—6". Evolution of a shell: These shells represent various stages in the growth of the conchiolin of a mollusk. The lip develops from a thickened flare into clawlike fingers. The mature animal continues to lay down conchiolin at the edge of its mantle even after its body has stopped growing. In this way, the lip grows larger and larger throughout the lifetime of the mollusk.

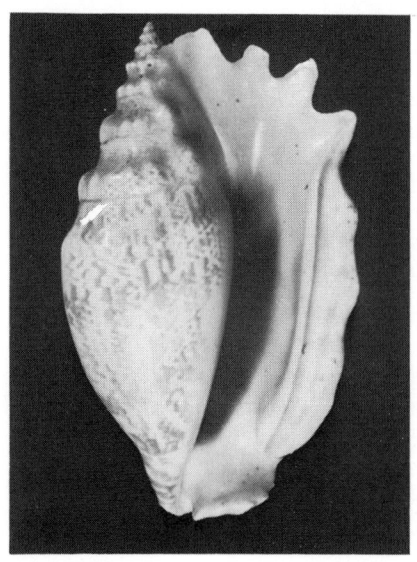 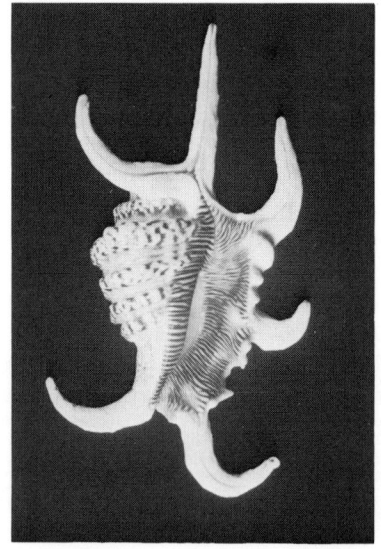

"grapes" are the egg cases of Squid. The Squid ends her maternal duties as soon as the eggs are laid, but the Octopus mother gives her young "tender, loving care." Octopus eggs are rarely seen, for they are suspended from the roof of the cave where the mother lives, in bunches of a few hundred to several thousand. Before each breeding season male Cephalopods grow an arm laden with spermatozoa. During mating, this arm breaks off within the body of the female, remaining there to fertilize the eggs as they are produced. The female Octopus is a self-sacrificing mother. Once her eggs are laid she remains with them, guarding them and waving her arms around them to keep the water circulating freely until they hatch out. It takes about 6 weeks for the eggs to hatch, and it is said that in all this time the mother Octopus will not leave her cave to find food.

A few fresh-water Bivalves have developed another method of avoiding the wastage caused by committing young to the plankton. Their larvae are parasitic, attaching themselves to the gills of passing fish and riding safely with their unwitting hosts until they grow big enough to live alone. Safely, that is, until their hosts are eaten by bigger fish, as frequently happens!

Snails which have developed partial independence of the water are less prodigal of their young. Those living far up on the shore mate like higher animals, incubate the eggs within their bodies, and retain the young until they develop shells. Each egg has an excellent chance of survival, as it is not subject to the vagaries of wind and tide for fertilization, food, and habitat. Mollusks that live far down on the shore, however, are still tied to the sea for reproduction; their breeding cycles are keyed to the spring tides, so that they release their spawn into the sea at the only time when it is available to them.

The trochophores of Bivalves and Univalves are very much alike; it is only during their veliger stage that certain changes take place within their bodies. They begin to make conchiolin, the material which will form their shells; and in the Gastropod veligers a radical change in body structure commences. Like the Bivalves, they hatch out with bodies that are bilaterally symmetrical. Soon, however, one side of their bodies continues to grow normally, while the other side slows its growth. The internal structure is altered, the stomach and organs forced out of their original position; slowly their bodies take on the twisted shape characteristic of Univalves.

How Shells Are Made

The young mollusks are still very tiny when they begin to form their shells. The shell material, conchiolin, is formed within their bodies, by complex organs that extract calcium and other minerals from their food. Conchiolin is a semi-

FLORIDA CROWN CONCH
Melongena corona—3"
The Florida Crown Conch is a scavenger and lives in brackish bays. Groups of Crown Conchs often "gang up" on other Snails, sitting in a circle around a chosen victim, and pouncing upon it when it opens its operculum to breathe.

EYED COWRIE
Cypraea argus—4"
This Cowrie is an excellent example of shell camouflage. Carotenoid and melanin pigments absorbed from the Cowrie's food are used by the mantle to make circles and blobs of color. These colors are not merely on the surface but extend throughout the thickness of the shell. However, the outer and inner layers of some shells, such as the Helmet Shell, from which cameos are cut, are of different hues.

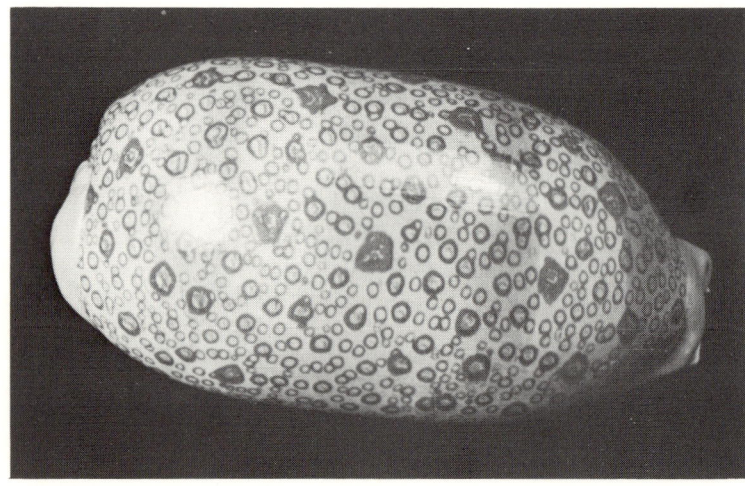

liquid substance that hardens rapidly when exposed to air or water. It is secreted and released by the delicate sac of tissue which covers the internal organs, the mantle, and most importantly by the mantle's edge. The shape of the finished shell depends on the shape of the mantle edge which made it. Spiked or ridged shells are made by species having mantles with frilled or ruffled edges; smooth shells are moulded by species with flat, regular mantle edges. Bivalve shells are formed by mantles divided into two lobes.

Conchs have very little mantle tissue (to lay down conchiolin) on the atrophied side of their bodies. The shell therefore becomes lopsided, twisted, spiralling around upon itself. As the mantle edge grows along with the body it covers, the shell grows also, so the animal never outgrows its shell. In some species, conchiolin goes on being secreted long after the mollusk has reached maturity and stopped growing. If the mantle edge stays in the same place and goes on secreting conchiolin, a thick "lip" builds up at the shell's growing edge, the outside edge of the aperture. Such a lip tells you that its builder probably lived to a ripe old age!

When carpenters need a strong, lightweight board they use plywood, made by adhering thin layers of veneer together with their grains at right angles, because they know that several thin sheets sandwiched together in this way are less likely to crack or split than one thick layer of wood. Mollusks use this principle in building their homes. Their shells are 3-ply, having an outer layer or epidermis, a middle layer, and a lining or inner layer. These layers can be compared to the walls of a house. The outer layer, the epidermis, is either horny or dull and whiskered; it serves to protect the softer layers within from acids in the water, just as siding protects insulation and inner walls from rain. The two inner layers are made of the same material—crystals of calcium carbonate—but they differ in appearance because of the way the crystals are laid down. The middle layer has horizontally placed crystals and looks dull and rough, as you can see if you examine a chipped or broken shell. The inner layer, however, has vertically placed crystals and a satin smooth finish that is beautiful to touch.

The porcelain smoothness of this inner layer is essential to the comfort of the owner of the shell, for the delicate mantle tissue resting against it would be chafed by the slightest roughness. Wherever mantle tissue touches the shell it deposits lining material or a similar substance; species such as Cowries which have outsized mantles overflowing their shells do not have a horny epidermis, but instead coat their outer surfaces with a hard, glossy material that protects them from chafing as well as from acid damage. Lining material continues to be produced so long as the animal lives—its shell never stops getting thicker. The two outer layers laid down by the growing edge of the mantle are usually quite thin; the bulk of the shell is lining material.

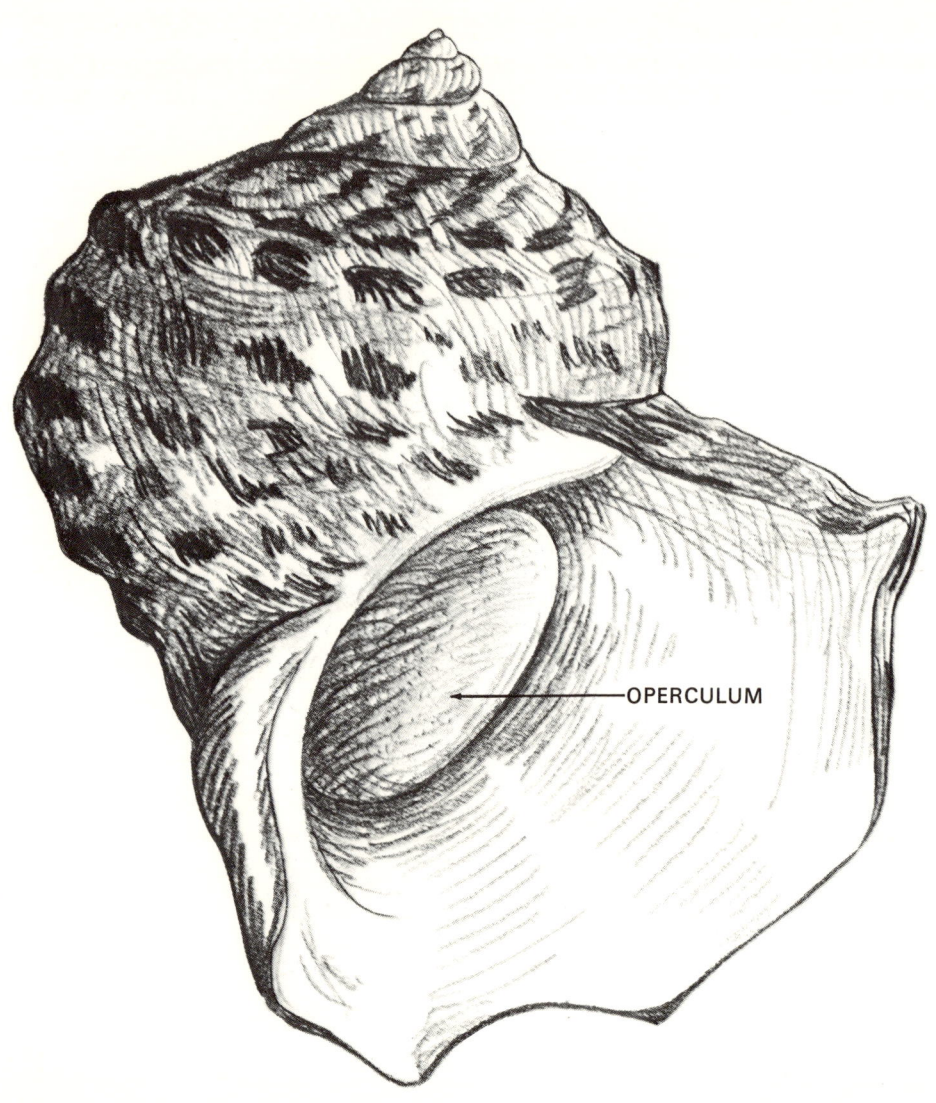

GREEN TURBAN showing Operculum
Turbo marmoratus—8"
The operculum is a limey plate on the base of the foot which, among other things, acts as a trapdoor for the living Snail. Some mollusks have a thin, horny operculum, many have none at all. This operculum was replaced in the shell after the death of the Snail.

As with human builders, cold weather slows down construction. The rate at which shell material is deposited depends upon the species, for some mollusks reach maturity more quickly than others; but it also varies with the temperature of the water, for calcium is more easily absorbed in warm than in cold waters. As you might expect, therefore, tropical mollusks tend to grow thicker shells than their cousins of colder regions. If a mollusk is subjected to wide changes in temperature its rate of growth will fluctuate, and during the periods of retarded growth the lip of its mantle will hardly grow at all. The shell material secreted during these periods builds up into a false lip, to be left behind when the animal starts growing again. Some species stop making conchiolin when they stop growing, leaving only a scar to mark the event when they recommence growth. In areas where there is a wide range between summer and winter temperature it is possible to estimate the age of shells by counting the number of false lips, or "varices" as they are called, or the number of scars, just as it is possible to count the age of a tree in the rings of its wood.

Occasionally, especially on rocky beaches, one will find a shell with a different kind of scar, the irregular mark left by a repair job. In areas where stones are tumbled onto mollusks or mollusks are beaten against rocks by the surf, injuries are frequent. The animal owner of a damaged shell can repair it with extra shell material, patching the break, but it is unable to hide the scar that results.

There are almost as many shapes and sizes of opercula, the little trapdoors that close the apertures of shells, as there are shapes and sizes of shells. Some opercula are formed in rings or ovals, while others are elongated or curved. A display of varieties is interesting and attractive, for some are quite pretty. The common Moon Snail, for example, makes an operculum that is tawny brown with silver or gold edges.

The Battle to Live

Every living thing is a link in the chain of food which commences with simple, one-celled animals and plants and ends in the highest forms of life. Mollusks are no exception, for they prey on the lower creatures and plants and are preyed on by higher animals and by man. Their lives, therefore, are a constant battle to eat and avoid being eaten.

Different mollusks obtain food in different ways. Some are herbivores, grazing on pastures of seaweed or scraping algae from the slime of the bottom. There are many carnivores. Scavengers help to clear away the decaying gobbets of flesh that litter its floor. Cannibals suffocate or tear smaller shellfish to pieces; assassins use poisoned daggers to kill their prey.

ROYAL COMB VENUS
Pitar dione—2"
The most beautiful of the American Venus Clams, the Royal Comb is found from Texas to the West Indies. This uncommon species is ivory-white, except for the base of the spines which are marked with violet and purple.

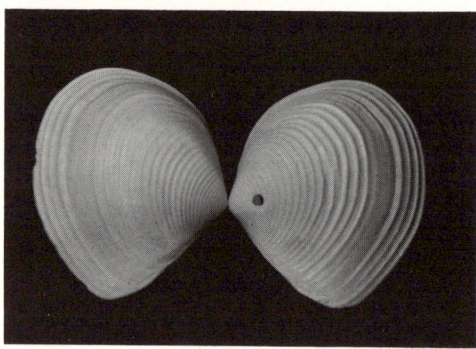

CHANNELED DUCK CLAM
Anatina plicatella—2½"
This Clam's bleached white shell is thin and fragile compared to other Clams. Its hinge bears a central spoonlike depression called a chondrophore. This specimen fell prey to a Snail, as evidenced by the drill hole.

All mollusks other than Bivalves possess a radula, a ribbon of chitinous teeth, and some species have more than three hundred rows of tiny teeth. A highly effective rasp, the radula is often assisted by acid secretions which soften the shell of the victim. This drill hole piercing the heavy shell of an Ark may have taken the attacking Snail many hours to complete.

Bivalves lead unexciting lives for the most part, living buried in mud or attached to stones. They are suspension feeders; that is, they feed by straining out minute animals and plants suspended in the water. In species which live deeply buried the mantle tissue has evolved into twin pipes or siphons, joined and encircled by a thin membrane, which protrude from their shells and stick up into the clear water above. Clamdiggers call these siphons "necks." A steady stream of water is drawn down through the incurrent siphon to bathe the gills of the mollusk below. Oxygen and food are extracted, waste material is given off, and the water returned to the sea via the other, excurrent siphon.

Some Bivalves have retractable siphons; in others, the siphons are too large to be retracted comfortably within the shell valves, which therefore have gaping margins at the point where the neck protrudes. Some varieties with this vulnerable shell modification are fast diggers. The neck protrudes permanently in some species, forming a siphonal snout.

Bivalves that live above ground do not need necks, and instead take in and pump out water through openings in their mantle tissue.

We once captured a Razor Clam and placed it in a tidepool. After a minute it opened its tightly shut valves, pushed its long foot into the mud, hauled itself into a vertical position, and disappeared like an elevator down a shaft. A Clam digs vertically much as a Snail moves horizontally; it pushes its foot down as far as possible, expands the tip of its foot to form an anchor, and then contracts its muscles to pull its body downward.

Some Bivalves are deposit feeders, sifting out food particles from the sediment on the bottom. These creatures use their siphons as a housewife uses a vacuum cleaner, running the nozzles, or orifices as they are more properly called, over the sea bed to suck in muddy water rich in tiny organisms. The Scallops and Lima Clams are deposit feeders that can move rapidly from place to place. A Lima Clam travels in a series of hops, using its muscular foot as a spring to push it up from the bottom; the Scallop is a true swimmer, opening and closing its valves rapidly to force out jets of water which push against the inertia of the water behind it and propel it forward.

These Bivalves escape their enemies by speed; others survive by entombing themselves alive. Piddocks bore into rock and Teredos (or Shipworms) into wood while they are young, forming tunnels with narrow openings too small to permit their passage later on.

How do Teredos drill holes in solid wood pilings? They have long, wormlike bodies with a built-in file—a pair of small valves covered with sharp, hard little teeth. These valves are placed against the wood and rocked to and fro by their owner's powerful adductor muscle. Rasplike, the teeth file the wood away, making a hole which deepens as the work continues and enlarges as the animal and its

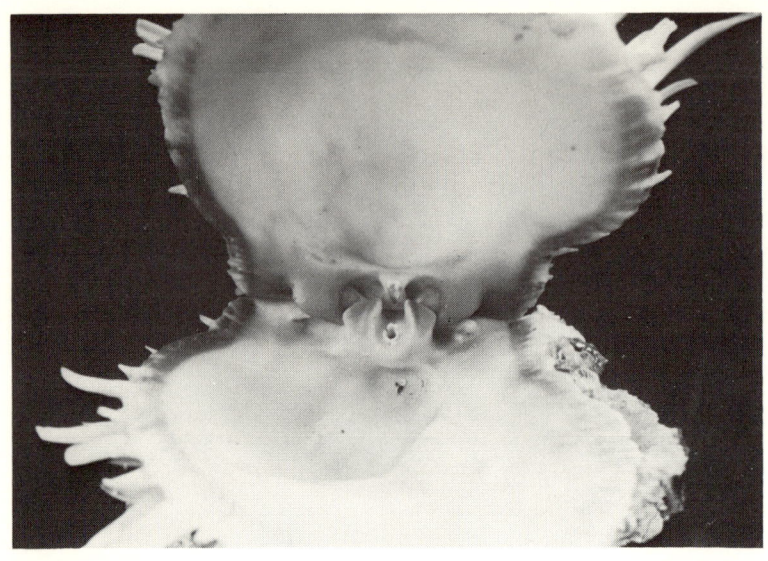

THORNY OYSTER
Spondylus americanus—4"
This intricate hinge, which operates like a ball and socket joint, together with a powerful adductor muscle, protects the Oyster from any attempt to wrench its valves apart.

SPINY COCKLE
Cardium aculeatum—3" - 4"
Some Bivalves
secure their castles
against the hungry world
with interlocking teeth.

32

toothed valves grow larger. Eventually the Shipworm's self-made cave may be 12 inches long and a quarter inch across.

People who are responsible for maintaining wooden piers and ships go to a great deal of trouble to protect the wood from Teredo infestation with paint, pitch, or metal sheathing, for once Teredos have entered it is difficult to get rid of them. Drydocking of ships is not completely successful, as the Shipworms can live for several weeks without water; however, they cannot live in fresh water. Rainy seasons, which decrease the salinity of seawater, decrease Teredo activity. Years ago little was done to protect wood from Teredos, though the sudden crumbling of apparently solid wood caused by these pests had been dreaded by sailors for centuries.

While the Shipworms and Piddocks live in their cells, entombed alive but safe, the rest of the Bivalves pass their lives in ever-present danger. When the tide submerges them they must thrust out their siphons to feed; the siphons themselves are tasty morsels for flatfish swimming in over the mud. At low tide, gulls dig them up and feast on them, carrying them high in the air and dropping them on rocks to break the valves apart. Bivalves are a staple food of higher mollusks and of Starfish, while man harvests certain kinds for seafood and other purposes. Oyster Drills and Moon Snails compete with us for our Oyster dinners; and while we have laws to protect the Oysters during their breeding season and when they are young, voracious Conchs know no law.

The Oyster Drills are well equipped for butchery. They possess a vicious array of teeth which they use to carve up their victims piecemeal, an enormous foot which is used for smothering, and eyes mounted on stalks to ensure maximum vision as they prowl the sea bed. Their teeth, embedded in a chitinous ribbon, are razor sharp and can be raised or lowered at will. The foot has a fleshy hump in front, like the cow-catcher on a train, that helps the animal plow its way through the mud in search of food.

When a Clam senses danger it pulls in its siphons and snaps its thick valves together, if it is able; our expressions "shut up like a clam" and "clam up" come from the sudden withdrawal which these creatures make when alarmed. The fortress-like shell baffles most aggressors, but the hungry Moon Snail calmly climbs onto the upper valve of its intended victim and settles down to bore a hole through to the flesh within. Some predators emit drops of acid to soften up the shell before the tooth ribbon, or radula, comes into play, but in most species the teeth perform the work unaided. Once the hole is completed, the Snail inserts its radula-tipped snout and scrapes away the flesh of the living clam piece by piece.

The Starfish is another danger to Bivalves. Lacking boring apparatus, it uses brute strength to obtain its food. Its arms, like those of the Octopus, are covered

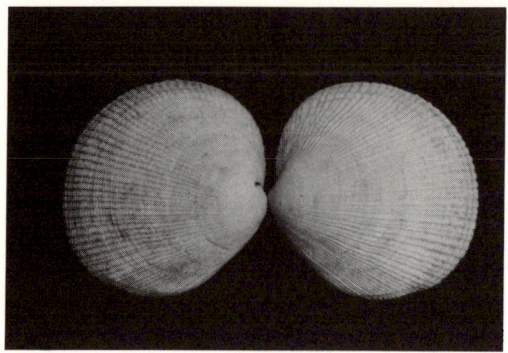

TIGER LUCINE
Codakia orbicularis—2½"
This American Lucine is a close relative of the Pacific Tiger, found half a world away. So finely sculptured its shell almost looks beaded, it also is easily recognized by the pink margins on the interior of the valves.

PENNSYLVANIA LUCINE
Lucina pennsylvanica—1½"
North Carolina south to the Caribbean. Dwelling in sand 3 feet below the surface, the Lucines construct a mucous-lined sand tube which serves in place of an incurrent siphon.

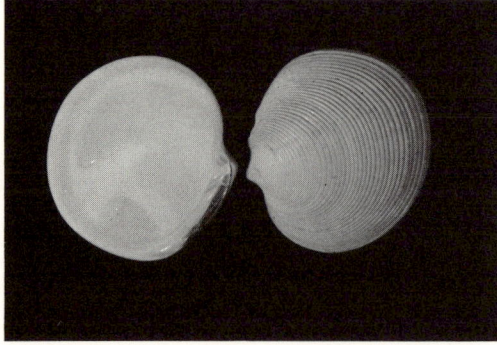

ELEGANT DOSINIA
Dosinia elegans—3"
Commonly found in the Caribbean and from Florida to Texas. Because the Dosinia cannot dig rapidly, many of the valves you will find washed up on beaches are scarred by drill holes—the marks of predatory Snails.

with powerful suction discs. Crawling up to a Clam, it presses several of these armlike rays against each valve to get a good grip with its suckers, and then begins a long, steady pull that finally overcomes the resistance of the Clam's adductor muscle and wrenches the valves apart. Unable to eat in the normal way because it has no teeth or grinding plates, the Starfish turns its stomach inside out, protrudes it through its mouth, and inserts the flabby bag between the gaping valves of the unlucky Clam. After its digestive juices have dissolved the meat, the Starfish pulls its stomach back inside its body and crawls away from its victim's empty shell.

A few Gastropods swallow smaller mollusks whole. These species have toothed plates in their stomachs that grind the shells of their prey to fragments. All mollusks have a similar digestive system, a simple tube enlarged along its length to form a throat and stomach, but modifications such as grinding plates are not uncommon.

Some species, such as Whelks, have definite preferences in diet; those in the habit of eating Mussels will ignore other convenient tidbits, while those on a steady diet of barnacles will refuse the fattest mussels. The food mollusks eat affects the color of their shells. Barnacle-fed Whelks make white shells, but Whelks on a diet of Mussels will secrete pink or black conchiolin. It is unlikely that diet is the sole cause of color, however; we have dug pink, yellow, and orange Tellins from a yard-square area of sandy mud in a bay in southern England. These Tellins, apparently all of the same species, could not have selected different foods as they are suspension feeders.

Dog Whelks, or Nassas, are scavengers as well as carnivores. They exist in vast numbers and consume great quantities of dead as well as living creatures. They are an important factor in keeping our littoral zones clean. We have seen them in Florida Gulf Coast bays in such numbers that they crawled on each other for want of room to walk on the bottom.

Although the Snail is the terror of the Bivalves, it has enemies of its own. It may be eaten by a Starfish, a Cephalopod, or even by a larger Snail. Like its victims the Clams, it defends itself by retreating into its shell at the first sign of danger and remaining passive until its enemy goes away. It cannot breathe properly with all its tissue packed into its shell, however, and finally must emerge or suffocate. Some cannibalistic Snails are aware of this; investigators report these larger Snails will wait in a circle around a small Snail until it is forced to come out for air. This gives them an opportunity to slip their toothed snouts through the aperture. Their victim snaps its operculum down tight, but the snouts are too tough to be hurt by the pinch. At last the beleaguered Snail must breathe again. When it relaxes, the waiting teeth reach the muscle that holds its operculum in place,

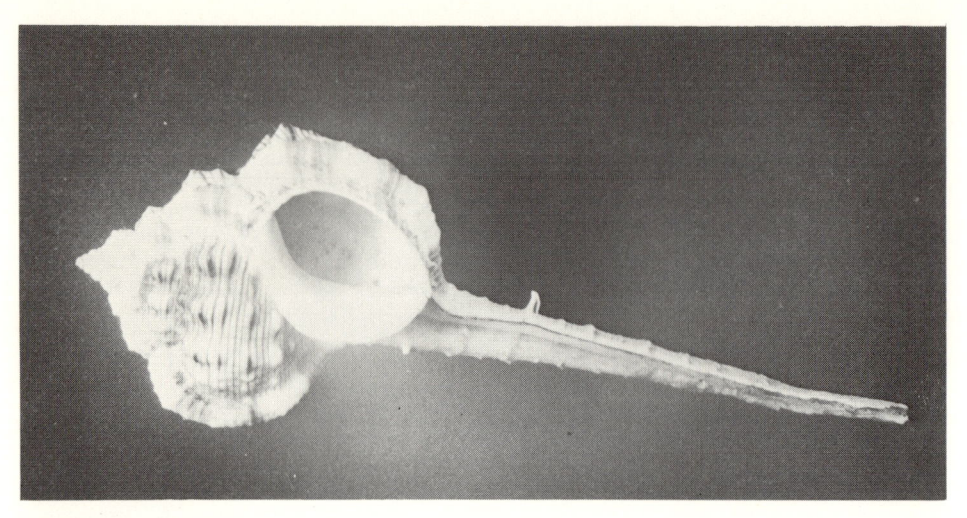

SNIPE'S BILL MUREX
Murex haustellum—5"
The spikes and ridges and elongated siphonal canal of the Murex are more than mere ornaments—they provide stability in rough seas by acting as anchors on muddy bottoms. Thus, their owners cannot be swept out to sea, away from their food supply or up on shore.

LACE MUREX
Murex florifer—2½"
Common in Florida, this delicate Murex is a carnivore. Using its powerful suction foot as a lever, and prying with its spiky outer lip, it can force open the shell of an Oyster or Clam. Its frilly outline allows it to blend in with the sea wrack and marine growths upon which it lives.

and saw away at it until the trapdoor falls free. Then they settle down to feast on their still living victim.

Large Conchs may choose to attack their enemies, wielding the sharp-edged, claw-like operculum at the tip of the foot as a sword. The Florida Queen Conchs use their trapdoors in this way, inflicting nasty cuts on unwary shell collectors. Mollusks cannot move their body mass very fast, so the sharp spikes and spines which adorn families like Thorny Oysters and Murex cannot be used in combat; but the Murex is reported to use its spines as a wedge to force open Clam shells.

Tropical Cone Shells have an even more effective method of hunting. They manufacture a deadly poison in the glands of their bodies. Each Cone has a saclike gland in its head where the poison is stored before use. Ducts connect the gland to hollow, harpoon-like teeth. When a Cone strikes its victim the poison runs out through the ducts and teeth into the wound, causing paralysis or death. There are well-documented accounts of shell collectors handling tropical Cones carelessly and receiving a bite which caused great pain followed by coma and death. Even though there are no deadly species around American shores, collectors recommend extreme caution in handling large (over 2-inch-long) specimens; they may not be killers, but they can still inflict a nasty bite. It is interesting to note that the Cone is not harmed by eating the poison-saturated body of its prey, though the venom is strong enough to kill a man hundreds of times its size and weight!

The poisoned daggers of the Cones serve as defensive as well as offensive weapons; Octopi and other larger creatures that see the Cone as an easy meal change their minds with the first stab, usually crawling away to die. Shell collectors the world over are undeterred, for Cones have beautiful shells. While many species are quite common, some are very rare; the Glory of the Seas Cone sells for as much as three thousand dollars.

All Univalves are not carnivorous, however. Limpets and Periwinkles are peaceable species common on many temperate shores. At low tide it is easy to find Periwinkles almost anywhere there is seaweed, though they must be looked for, as they like to cluster together in groups beneath the dead-looking fronds of dried-out weed. As the tide rises, little air bladders in this decrepit mass float it out, and suddenly it is no longer dull and lifeless but shining and translucent, glowing with a hundred subtle tones of brown and green and red. Its fronds are lifted to the surface by the air bladders so that it can obtain food by photosynthesis, that is, use of the sun's energy to transform substances it gets from the water into a form it can use.

Seaweed has much in common with the green and growing plants in our gardens. The floating weed forms a submarine forest, and the Periwinkles emerge from their shells to graze on the algae growing around the holdfasts, the roots of the kelp and eelgrass we call "wrack," that grows in the sea and is cast up on shore at high tide. Periwinkles do such a good job of keeping algae eaten down that Oyster farmers sometimes gather them by the bucketful to drop on the Oyster beds, hoping the Winkles will eat algae that might otherwise smother young Oysters.

The Periwinkles have rounded shells and are easily washed from the rock by the tide, so they seek crevices and other sheltered places to live in. The flat, exposed surfaces are colonized primarily by Limpets, who can survive in such places because of their flattened, conical shells which sit recessed in grooves worn into the rock, and their powerful suction-disc foot. A Limpet begins work on its homesite as soon as it settles to the bottom at the end of its veliger stage; it attaches itself to a stone with its suction disc and rubs its shell to and fro. The friction wears away the rock and also the edge of the shell, so the Limpet must secrete enough conchiolin to replace the material worn away, as well as to extend its shell to fit its growing body. As time goes by, the circular groove in the rock gets deeper and larger, giving its owner increased protection against the pounding waves.

Gulls find Limpets easy prey at low tide, swooping down and knocking them from their homesites before the unlucky mollusks realize their danger. While the breakers of the falling or rising tide are tugging at them, the Limpets clamp down firmly to keep from being swept away, but at low tide they relax, keeping a little water in their shells so the sun and dry air will not harm their moisture-loving bodies. Once submerged, they creep from their homesites to forage, often travelling far from home in search of food. They seem to know when the falling tide will endanger them and find their way unerringly to their homesites before the breakers strike. Scientists have tried to fool Limpets by moving them while feeding, cutting grooves into the rock between them and their homesites, and chipping the homesites so they would no longer fit their owners' shells; but the Limpets were not to be fooled. Somehow they knew their way home, crawled past the man-made obstacles, and settled down to regrind their damaged homesites. A great deal was learned about what they can do, but very little about how they do it!

The two smallest molluscan groups live peaceable lives also. The Scaphopoda are mud dwellers, taking food from the sea by means of hairlike cilia protruding from their shells, while the Amphineura are vegetarians like Limpets. The food habits of Cephalopods, however, are interesting.

Octopi are untidy creatures that leave the empty shells of the mollusks and crabs they eat in undersea "kitchen middens" (see page 74), heaped before their caves. They like to live in dark places, and in the absence of natural rock shelters build homes of their own by heaping up piles of debris and scooping out holes in them. Although they lack the armorplate of their more attractive kin, their armament puts most mollusks to shame. Octopi have powerful offensive weapons: the suckers that cover their tentacles, and horny, parrotlike beaks capable of shearing through almost anything. Octopi are intelligent animals, and stories of their behavior are legion. It is said that they hypnotize or fascinate crabs into walking into their mouths, and keep a larder of victims imprisoned in a fold of the mantle connecting their arms until they have enough for a feast, instead of eating them as snacks as they are caught! Having once failed to open a Clam, an Octopus does not repeat the experiment, but waits for the Clam to open up to breathe and then thrusts a stone between the valves so they cannot close. Then it wrenches the valves apart and makes a leisurely meal.

Octopi eat enormous quantities of lobsters and crabs, and thus come into conflict with man. They often crawl into lobster pots to eat the trapped lobsters within, only to find themselves caught in their turn and at the mercy of an angry fisherman whose catch they have destroyed. They too have many enemies. Conger eels, cod, and other large sea creatures harass them, while sperm whales and sharks are always on the lookout for their tasty cousin, the Squid. The Squid have one defensive weapon besides their wonderful camouflage: the ability, when pursued, to emit a cloud of blackish ink which provides a smokescreen, hiding them while they escape. This ink is pure sepia, the pigment from which the rich brown ink used by artists is derived. The ink of the Cuttlefish, when dried, is another source of sepia.

Very few creatures of the sea die of old age, though authorities say an Oyster can live for 30 years, a Clam about 20, and a large Conch perhaps 25. The need for protection in a savage world has led to the evolution of some weird forms of camouflage. One Gastropod, the Carrier Shell, cements bits of stone and broken shell onto its back. This odd-looking pile of rubbish moving slowly along the bottom must discourage most hunters. Of all the enemies which mollusks face, however, the most relentless is surely man. Against this adversary the Cone's poison and the Carrier's camouflage are no defense.

Some unthinking commercial enterprises are making novelties from small shells which were harvested before they grew large enough to produce even one batch of eggs. This wanton overcollection has put many once-common species on a downhill road that may lead to their extinction. The odds against young mollusks are heavy; a new toll can turn the scales against them. California had to protect the lovely Abalones of the Pacific Coast with laws to control their harvesting. Similar laws are needed to ensure that many of the Atlantic seaboard species will be there when our children walk the beaches of the future.

CROSS-BARRED VENUS
Chione cancellata—1"
South Carolina southward. This perfectly sculptured Venus has radial ribs, prominent concentric ridges, and an interior commonly a rich purple.

PERFECT SPECIMENS

SHUTTLE SHELL
Volva volva—4"
The most perfect shell specimens, as experienced collectors know, are found on live mollusks. This Shuttle Shell is a perfect, glossy, unmarred specimen. Rolling in breakers, beating against rocky shores, and bleaching in the sun—all combine to wear and chip the ridges and striations, resulting in a "dead" shell.

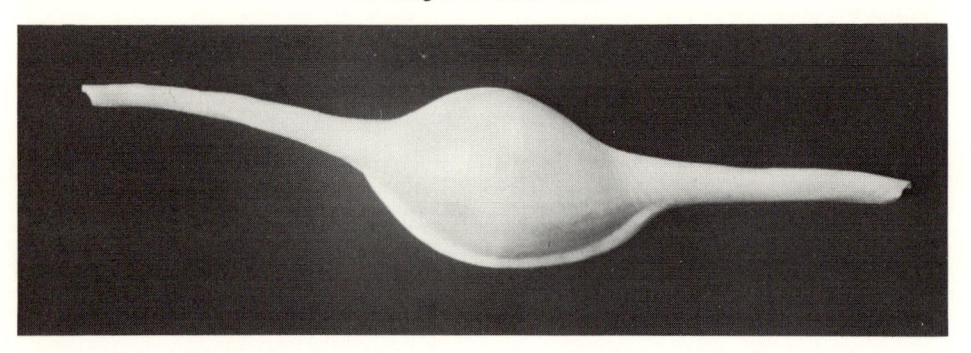

3 Collecting Mollusks

Finding Perfect Specimens

NOW THAT YOU HAVE LEARNED something of the lives of the shell dwellers you will find a greater interest in the shells you already have or will collect. Shell hunting is fun: every stretch of beach teems with hidden life; every weed-covered rock may hide a beautiful or rare species you have never seen before. But a good collection is not easy—it results from many hours of happy hunting, and a little planning. To pick up beachworn shells is easy, but after a time you will find yourself looking at them critically, and wanting better specimens. The most perfect shells are found on living mollusks, and the search for them has all the fascination and thrill of a treasure hunt.

Most shell collector's handbooks start with a list of things to take along on shelling expeditions. It would be interesting to add up the weights of all these pieces of gear, and see how far one could stagger under the load! Although there are accessories which are helpful for certain purposes, the only thing you really have to have is a bag to carry your shells in—one that will not fall apart when it gets wet. It helps, too, to carry a small box filled with cotton, for fragile shells; it is heartbreaking to find a delicate, perfect specimen and then have it crushed to fragments on the way home.

In rocky areas a pointed bar (pinch bar), for turning over stones, and a pocket knife for prying mollusks off rocks will be useful. A shovel and a bucket, or a can that will hold water, are necessary when hunting Clams that live buried in mud. Tongue depressors or similar flat strips of wood, together with lengths of soft string, are needed for Chiton hunting. Most shell collectors keep these simple tools in their cars, to have them handy, leaving them in the trunk until needed. Whatever the old manuals may say, you don't have to drag along a pickaxe every time you walk down a beach!

There is one other accessory which will be a great help to you: a glass-bottomed box or bucket with the inside painted black. The surface of the sea is rarely

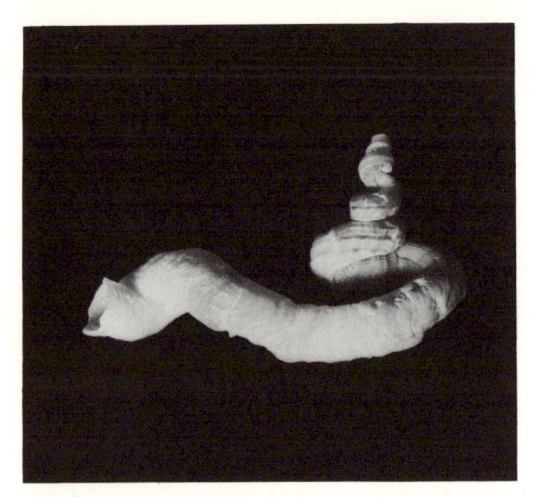

WEST INDIAN WORM SHELL
Vermicularia spirata—3"
Florida Keys to the West Indies. This Worm Shell leads a solitary life. Some other varieties attach themselves to rocks or twine inextricably together to form colonies.

COMMON ATLANTIC SLIPPER SHELL
Crepidula fornicata—1"-1½"
Slipper Shells live in shallow water in colonies, often attached to one another in piles. As they mature, the young males release a hormone into the water which causes the males underneath them to undergo a sex change, and they become females.

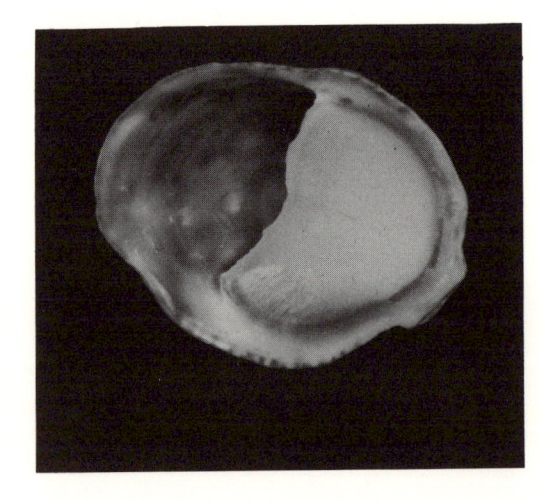

smooth, for even the smallest breeze causes ripples, making a bewildering dance of light and shade. Trying to see the bottom through this is like trying to see through a frosted glass window. A glass-bottomed box, floated on the water, gives a porthole view of the sea bed. You can make the box yourself, or buy it fairly cheaply from a marine supply company. A skin-divers' face mask for surface use is a fair substitute, but the rippling water around it causes glare and distraction and it has a very limited viewing area.

Experienced collectors plan their shelling trips to coincide with the lowest of low tides. Tables listing the times of high and low tide are published in the newspapers of coastal towns. At low tide, Bivalves are left stranded on the beach by the retreating water, to be had for the taking by birds and collectors alike. The Univalves are always harder to find; abandoned by the water, they creep into tidepools and bury themselves in mud, or hide under seaweed. They leave only a little of their shells sticking out of the mud, and are quite hard to spot. Float the viewing box in a tidepool and look for little bumps on its bottom; then prod, and you may come up with a buried Snail!

As the tide falls it leaves piles of driftwood and rubbish behind. Lift the pieces up and look them over. Crumbling wood may contain Teredos. Wharf pilings and stone piers are exposed at low tide; they provide homes for many kinds of shell dwellers. Float your box in shallow water and look for tracks in the sand. Short, wide tracks are made by Sand Dollars and long, wandering ones by horseshoe crabs; but if you find a trail that is fairly short and ends in a little hummock you may have found a Moon Snail. Poke the mound gently and he will move away, still buried. A bump on the bottom that moves along slowly indicates a Conch on the prowl.

Scavenging mollusks have a keen sense of smell. If you are patient you might try anchoring a bit of rotten meat to a stone in shallow, quiet water and waiting to see if there are visitors. The aroma travels a good distance under water, and will attract large numbers of scavengers if they are anywhere about.

Shells you want to keep should go into your bag at once. If you pile them on the beach while you look for more you may find your choicest specimens have walked away! This is because empty mollusk shells do not always remain empty: the hermit crab, a lazy little animal that will not bother to build a home of his own, often moves in. It is quite a surprise to pick up an apparently empty shell, and then see long, horny legs sliding out of its aperture! In some shallow, muddy bays it seems there are more shells harboring hermit crabs than shells containing mollusks. This is not surprising, as shells last for many years after their builders die and there are vast numbers of hermit crabs around to occupy them. The hermits have soft, defenseless tails which they protect with the borrowed armor.

ANGEL WING
Barnea costata—5"
Living in deep mudflats, one to three feet beneath the surface, these shells are among the most beautifully sculptured known. Most specimens are pure white. Overcollection had led to the near-extinction of the uncommon pink form.

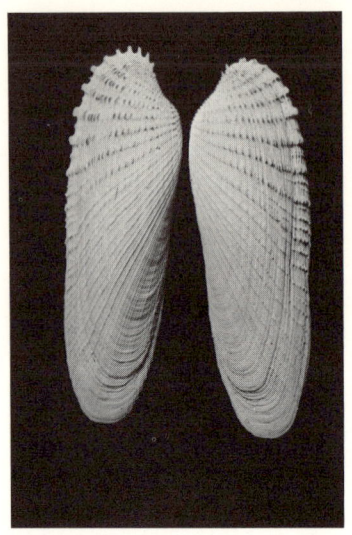

FALSE ANGEL WING
Petricola pholadiformis—2"
Although bearing a close resemblance to the True Angel Wing, it is much smaller and bores its way into clay or peat in the intertidal zone.

LONG-SPINED STAR SHELL
Astraea phoebia—2"
Hunt for this Star Shell in shallow, grassy bays and on eelgrass in the Florida Keys. The periostracum, or exterior, of the shell is either brownish yellow or greenish, and the interior is a pearl color. Specimens vary—this one has shorter than average spines. Some have an elongated spine, and an umbilicus.

A tiny hermit finds a tiny empty shell, backs his soft tail in and settles down, anchoring his tail around the columella. When he grows too big for the shell he finds a larger one, takes a careful look round for enemies, and then slips out of the old and into the new home as quickly as he can. If you pick up an apparently empty shell and hear a sharp clicking sound, you have heard a hermit crab pulling in his claws. Set the shell down, stand back, and wait quietly; in a few minutes your shell will saunter off!

Mollusks usually move fairly slowly on land, or are too timid to come out of their shells at all when taken from the water; even so, it is best to put them in the bag promptly, for the one you most want to keep is sure to be the one that disappears!

The mud flats and sand bars exposed at low tide are pitted with holes leading to buried clams, crabs, and worms. Deciding which hole leads to which animal is quite a problem. Worms often leave casts of mud at their doors, or build tubes covered with bits of broken shell and tiny stones that stick up an inch or so above the sand. Other holes may not display these nameplates, but digging will turn up only a large, vividly colored sea worm, or a crab. The only way to be sure a Clam made a particular hole is to see its siphons. It is easy to see siphons when there is water over them, but as the tide falls the necks are retracted underground. If you try to dig up a Clam when there is water above it you will stir up huge clouds of mud and the hole will fill in as you dig it; the only thing to do is to try to remember where you saw the necks and dig later, when the sand is high and dry.

If you are lucky and persevering enough to get one of the fragile Angel Wings (*Barnea Costata*), or any other delicate-valved Clam, it must go into a bucket of sea water at once, or it will contract violently and shatter its shell to pieces.

If you find sun-bleached Olive Shells or Coquinas in the debris on the beach you will know there are colonies living nearby. These mollusks are very common on sandy beaches around southern U.S. coastlines, living buried just beneath the surface. A little shallow digging may turn up hundreds of them. Try taking along a kitchen colander one day, shoveling mud into it, and then swirling it in the sea to wash away the mud; you may be surprised at what you have sieved out!

Sea grasses on mudflats shelter large numbers of shell dwellers, just as seaweed and kelp do in rocky areas. Wade or row out and look among the roots as well as on the stems. Pull up a frond or two; some species like to cling around the holdfasts. We once found thousands of little green Nerites just below the water line on reeds in a Mississippi Gulf Coast bay. Along the southern U.S. Atlantic coastline the beautiful Star Shells can be found, clinging to blades of kelp. Mangrove roots submerged at high tide harbor Coon Oysters, and the Conchs which feed on them; high in the mangrove branches are Snails making the transition from sea to land. If you have a boat, try drifting in the shallow water above mud-flats and fishing around with a long-handled rake. Hard-shell Clams are sometimes collected in this way.

Dredging for shells is a pleasant way to spend an afternoon. Your dredge may be an expensive professional job installed aboard a yacht. But it can also be a home-made bag of chicken wire, supported and held open at the neck by coat hangers bent into a rectangle, and towed behind a rowboat with a length of clothesline! In shelling, simple tools get excellent results.

Every rocky coast hides an abundance of life. High on the shore are species that breathe air and drown if they are immersed in water for very long. These creatures stand dry air and lack of moisture well, drying out and becoming comatose if necessary until wet weather or high tides revive them. (There are many stories of Periwinkles accidentally left uncleaned coming to life after years in display cabinets; we found one crawling around a tool shed three months after we collected it and stored it as an empty shell.)

Living farther down on the rocks are mollusks which require a daily bath if they are to survive. Even closer to the low-tide mark, species dry out and die in a few hours of strong sunlight; species living below the low-water mark cannot stand the sun at all, and die in an hour or two if they are not submerged. The underside of stones in these areas has a rich coating of weeds and algae that makes a pleasant habitat for shell dwellers. When stones are overturned and not replaced, the sunlight destroys this growth, and mollusks cannot shelter there for months, until it grows again. So when you move rocks, replace them as they were. Next year you may want to collect in that area again!

Lift up and look among the fronds of seaweed. Some Snails are so perfectly camouflaged that you may have trouble seeing them when you are looking directly at them. All the Amphineura (Chitons) live on rocks. They attach themselves very firmly, and you will have to use a knife to remove them. As you slide one from the rock, slip a wet tongue-depressor under it and tie it to the wood with string. This is important because otherwise the Chiton will roll up into a ball, and a rolled-up Chiton does not make a good collection specimen. If it does manage to curl up, drop it into the bucket of salt water and try again after it relaxes and straightens out. A Chiton in a bucket is wary, however, and curls at the first disturbance; it is far easier to tie it flat to begin with.

A word of warning here about collecting in areas where steep cliffs fall to the sea. In such areas there may be no beach uncovered at high tide, and the water may rise to considerable depth at the base of the cliffs. Every year visitors forget the CAUTION signs usually posted by the steps giving access to the beach. They wander too far to get back before the rising tide cuts them off, and spend hours on narrow strips of sand or sit cramped on rock ledges waiting for the tide to recede. In places where the cliff rises sheer and is swept by breakers at high tide they may drown. It is easy to lose track of time when you are far out on the rocks hunting shells and having fun, so check the tide-tables in the paper before starting, to be sure the tide is falling, not rising, and allow yourself plenty of time to get back.

Rocks on California coastlines may harbor Abalones. These creatures, like Limpets, have a suction-disc foot to secure them to the rock and must be pried loose with your knife blade. Abalones have a wide range; in Australia they are known as Mutton Fish, and in England the local species are called Ormers, or Ear Shells. The European species have the same shape and pearly lining as American, but they are much smaller. Abalones are protected by California law against overcollection; size and weight limits vary for different species, so check the current regulations in the area in which you plan to hunt them.

In some areas the shells you take, like the rocks they are found on, are covered with small, white, shell-like cones. These are barnacles; in spite of the shell-like covering they are not mollusks. For centuries educated people thought the long stemmed or "goose" barnacles were the eggs of migratory birds!

Harbors have large populations of wood- and rock-boring mollusks, but they are poor hunting places because their waters are full of decaying refuse, and are highly acid; the acid pits and dulls the shells exposed to it, making good specimens hard to find. Harbor bottoms have large scavenger populations which live on the refuse.

Florida fishermen sometimes catch Scallops by accident. If a line happens to fall between the open valves of a Scallop, the valves snap closed, and the Scallop can be drawn from the water attached to the line. It is doubtful that a collector would have such luck; dragging a home-made dredge behind a boat in shallow water would almost certainly get better results than dangling a line on the off-chance of its touching a Scallop.

Coral reefs are home to a wide variety of shell dwellers. The water around them is very clear, and if you look in the crevices and pools with a glass-bottomed box you may get some fascinating glimpses of underwater life. It is worthwhile to walk out to the edge of the reef when the tide is low. Those who have looked down through fathoms of crystal-clear blue, over the slopes of living coral that fall sharply away to unseen depths, will not soon forget the unique, mysterious beauty of the undersea world. The sea has always exercised a strange fascination on men; here at its portals this attraction can be felt most keenly. Only the skin-diver can know the reef fully, visiting the living world beneath the surface and returning to tell others of the experience.

The reef is very generous to visitors who cannot swim among its denizens, however. It is honeycombed with submarine tunnels and caves, which interconnect with the surface pools and rivers. Sitting beside these pools one can watch schools of tiny, gay-hued fish, baby Octopi at play, and the undulating progress of the beautiful Nudibranch mollusks. These animals have no external shell and lose their colors when taken from the water, so there is no reason for anyone interested in shells to capture them. If they are alarmed they hunch like garden slugs, drawing their lovely gill plumes into the safety of their bodies and becoming colorless, so that they look like lumps of greyish jelly. The sea anemones they eat also do this. Sea anemones are curious animals; with their bodies relaxed they look like flowers. It is a surprise to try to pick what looks like a chrysanthemum out of a tidepool, only to have it turn into a blob of wrinkled jelly!

The beautiful petals of the sea anemone are not innocent: they are tentacles, capable of inflicting paralyzing stings on small fish that come within their reach. Once the fish is helpless the tentacles seize it and guide it down to the mouth waiting hidden under those pretty petals. Sea anemones attach themselves to rocks and empty shells impartially; if a hermit crab comes along and moves into the shell, so much the better for all concerned. In this odd partnership the crab is hidden from its enemies by the flower above, and the anemone is carried from place to place and gets more food than a stationary existence would provide. The Nudibranchia eat sea anemones, assimilate their stings in some way, and store them in lobes of their bodies until needed. It is said that they can release these stings.

When you are exploring a coral reef, be careful. Potholes and tidepools are hard to tell apart in the clear water; you may start to wade across what you think is a shallow pool and find yourself out of your depth without warning. The coral is razor sharp, so it is wise to wear thick-soled shoes and handle it carefully. Some of the creatures living on reefs have poisonous spines hard enough to pierce a thin-soled sandal. The light which bounces off white coral and sparkling water can cause a bad sunburn, even on a less than perfect summer day, so it is best to wear clothes that afford some protection. Shorts and sleeveless tops are ideal for shell hunting in most areas, but not for coral. This tip comes from personal, painful experience!

Skin-diving is a wonderful way to collect fine specimens, if you are a good swimmer. Sponge-divers in many places, especially Greece and Florida, pick up rare and lovely deep water mollusks as they walk along the sea bed looking for sponges.

In clear shallow water, shelling from a boat is rewarding; if you have trouble seeing through the ripples and reflections, a glance through the glass-bottomed

BLUE-RAYED LIMPET
Helium pellucidium—$\frac{1}{2}$"-1"
An example of camouflage. This Limpet settles on the fronds of large seaweeds which are similarly marked. As it grows older it loses the blue streaks, thickens its shell, moves down to the rounded stalks of the seaweed, and builds up the edge of its shell to suit its rounded homesite. This specimen is from England.

LIMPET (interior)
Patella (Celana)—$\frac{3}{4}$"
Species from Casablanca, Africa. The rough exterior of this Limpet's shell belies its glossy, smooth interior.

GREEN STAR SHELL
Astrae tuber—1"-2"
Look for these on coral reefs or rocks, well camouflaged with an "overcoat" of sea moss and weed. Florida.

STRIPED FALSE LIMPET
Siphonaria pectinata—1"
East Florida and Texas to Mexico. These are very similar in appearance to the True Limpets *(Acmaea)*.

49

(Left)
BLEEDING TOOTH NERITE
Nerita peloronta—1"-1½"
Florida to Brazil. Found on rocks above and between tidelines.

(Right)
TESSELLATE NERITE
Nerita tessellata—½"
Florida to Texas and the Caribbean. Found in rock pools below the high tide mark. Some specimens are very dark.

COMMON FIG SHELL
Ficus communis—3"-4"
This shell, like the Giant Tun, (left, below) is often found intact on Florida's Gulf Coast shores; its light weight allows it to float and be tossed onto the beach while thicker, sturdier shells are destroyed in the surf.

GIANT TUN
Tonna galea—5"-7"
This specimen came from Corinth, Greece, and was brought in by sponge fishermen. Though light and fragile, the Tun is often washed up on the beach intact; it tends to float and be thrown high on the shore, while heavier shells are pounded to fragments in the surf. Found also from North Carolina to Texas, in the Pacific, and in the Mediterranean.

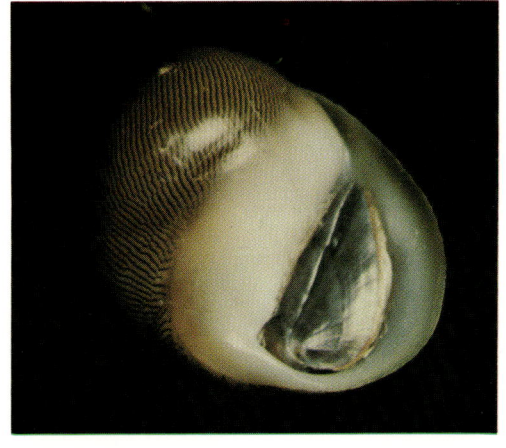

OLIVE NERITE
Neritina reclivata—to ½"
Note bluish operculum with orange border. These mollusks like to live on the stems of eelgrass in muddy bays. Florida. Hunt for them from a boat.

(Left) DELTOID ROCK SHELL. *Thais deltoidea*—1". Florida to West Indies. (Top right) ZIGZAG PERIWINKLE. *Littorina ziczac*—½". Florida to Caribbean. These fragile-shelled Periwinkles are common in rock crevices between tide lines. (Bottom right) EMERALD NERITE. *Smaragdia viridis*—⅕". Florida Keys to Brazil. Common on eelgrass in shallow bays.

HAITIAN TREE SNAIL
Liguus fasciatus—2"
This beautiful shell will die if moved to a different kind of tree from that on which it lives.

WEST INDIAN BUBBLE
Bulla occidentalis—⅘"
North Carolina to Caribbean. You can find Bubble shells on eelgrass growing in muddy bays.

TURRET SHELL
Turritella terebra—4"-5"
Indo-Pacific. Likes shallow water and muddy bottoms. The Turritellidae are related to the northern Periwinkles.

ORANGE SPIDER CONCH
Lambis crocata—4"
Indo-Pacific only.

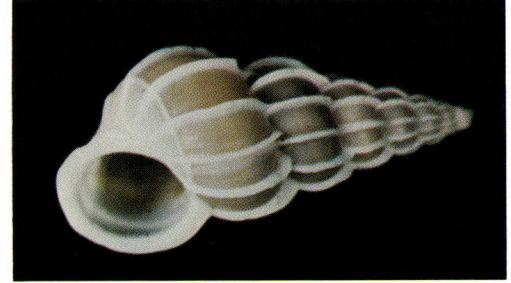

FLORIDA FIGHTING CONCH
Strombus alatus—3"-4"
Very common in Florida. Albino specimens are occasionally found on the Gulf coast of Florida. Sometimes freaks develop spines in place of the knobs on each whorl.

LAMELLOSE WENTLETRAP
Epitonium lamellosum—1"
Florida and Caribbean. Wentletrap comes from the Dutch word meaning "circular staircase."

**(Top)
SILVER CONCH**
Strombus lentiginosus—3"
Indo-Pacific.

**(Below)
BAT or VESPER VOLUTE**
Aulica vespertilio—3"
Indo-Pacific. The living Volute has a huge foot with which it can partially cover and protect its smooth and porcelainous shell.

CONCHS
This boy has been diving for Conchs off the coast of Yucatan, Mexico.

STRIPED BONNET
Phalium strigatum—3"
This specimen is from Okinawa. Range: Indo-Pacific.

53

EUROPEAN COWRIES (above)
Trivia europea—⅜"
One specimen cut to show interior structure. Found in sandy bays, shallow water.

LYNX COWRIES (left)
Cypraea lynx—1½"-2½"
Indo-Pacific. Two specimens showing the range of marking. Some are more distinctly spotted.

MONEY COWRIES (on left)
Cypraea moneta—1"
Indo-Pacific. At one time strings of these Cowries would be the purchase price of a slave—or a bride!

MIDGET HARP (top right of picture on left)
Harpa amouretta—1½"-2"
An attractive Pacific species.

HARP SHELL (right)
Harpa conoidalis—to 4"
Indo-Pacific.

HUMP BACK COWRIE
(top side, left—underside, right)
Cypraea mauritiana—3"
Indo-Pacific. The common name of this shell is derived from a hump on its back. This specimen is from Moluccas, Indonesia.

RETICULATED COWRIE (left)
Cypraea arabica reticulata—1½"-3¼"
Indo-Pacific.

TIGER COWRIE (left, below)
Cypraea tigris—2½"-5"
This specimen came from New Caledonia, but Tiger Cowries are abundant throughout the entire Indo-Pacific region.

(Below)
Cutaway view of a Tiger Cowrie shell, showing its spiral construction.

55

EGG SHELLS (above, left and right)
Ovula ovum—to 4"
Indo-Pacific. Strangely enough, the mantle which makes this shell porcelain-white is itself velvet black in hue! Egg shells are close relatives of the Cowries.

PURPLE SEA SNAILS (right and below)
Janthina janthina—1½"
The beautiful, fragile Janthina is pelagic, building a float of air bubbles trapped in mucous secretion to buoy it up. It spends its life on the surface of the ocean, and cannot survive contact with the shore.

SUNDIAL SHELL (right)
Architectonia nobilis—1"-1½"
Southeastern United States and Caribbean. Found in sand or mud.

TRITON'S TRUMPET
Charonia variegata—12"-18"
The Caribbean species is used in Peru during religious services as a musical instrument. In the South Seas, empty shells of the Pacific variety *(Charonia nobilis)* are used as cooking vessels, and in Japan are made into trumpets which Shinto priests use to call the faithful to prayer.

KING HELMET
Cassis tuberosa—6"
Because these Helmet Shells are constructed of layers of variously colored shell material, they are used for the carving of cameos. The cameo is carved to stand out in relief against the dark background layer.

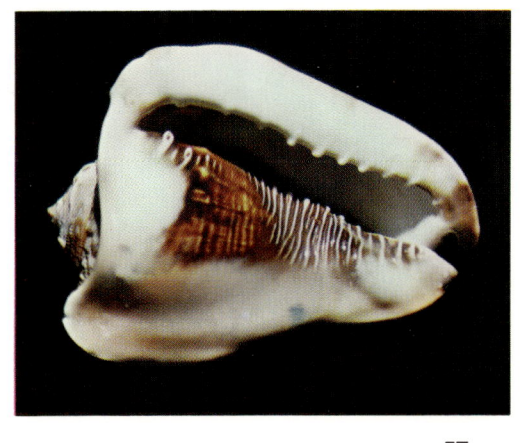

RAMOSE MUREX
Murex ramosus—to 10"
Indo-Pacific. Shallow water.

PINK-MOUTHED MUREX
Murex erythrostomus—to 6"
California south to Pacific coast of Central America. Lives in colonies on sandy mud bottoms.

APPLE MUREX
Murex pomum—2"-4½"
Southeastern United States and the Caribbean. Shallow water; common.

LIGHTNING WHELK or LEFT-HANDED WHELK
(Above, left)
Busycon contrarium—to 16"
Southeastern United States and Texas. Most shells are right-handed.

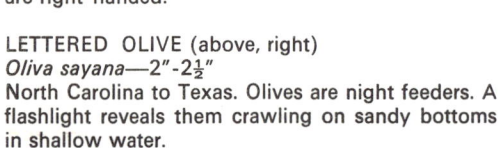

LETTERED OLIVE (above, right)
Oliva sayana—2"-2½"
North Carolina to Texas. Olives are night feeders. A flashlight reveals them crawling on sandy bottoms in shallow water.

BANDED TULIP (left)
Fasciolaria hunterea—3"
Southeastern United States.

TRUE TULIP (right)
Fasciolaria tulipa—4"
North Carolina south to the Caribbean.
The Tulips are carnivores. Look for them in shallow bays, on sand or weed.

NUTMEG
Cancellaria reticulata—1"-1¾"
Shallow water. North Carolina to Florida.
Albino specimens occasionally found.

BISHOP'S MITER (right)
Mitra mitra (formerly *Mitra episcopalis*)—to 5"
There are almost 600 species of Miters. The family name comes from the shell's resemblance to liturgical headgear. Indo-Pacific.

PAPAL MITER (right, below)
Mitra papalis—4"
Uncommon. Indo-Pacific.

TAPESTRY TURBAN
Turbo pentolatus—3"
This mollusk is an herbivore and grazes on coral reefs. The familiar blue-green "cat's eyes" brought home by tourists to the Pacific area are the opercula made by Tapestry Turbans.

59

TEXTILE CONE (left)
Conus textile—2"-4"

MARBLE CONE (right)
Conus marmoreus—2"-4"
These pretty Cones are common in Indo-Pacific waters.

CHINESE ALPHABET CONE
Conus spurius atlanticus—2"-3"
Southeastern United States. Shallow water.

MARLINSPIKE
Terebra maculata—to 10"
Common in tropical shallows. A large and showy species, common throughout the Indo-Pacific region. They are also called Auger or Screw Shells because of their multiple whorls.

CHAMBERED NAUTILUS
Nautilus pompilius—8"
The Nautilus is often stripped of its outer layer to reveal the nacre below, or bisected to show the sealed-off chambers within. The animal, a Squid, is carnivorous, hunting shellfish and crabs on the ocean floor. Over 60 small tentacles carry prey to its mouth.

TURKEY WING
Arca zebra—2"-3"
Turkey Wing Shells anchor themselves to rocks with strands of byssus, as mussels do.

RED ABALONE
Haliotis rufescens—to 10"
Best known for its mother-of-pearl lining which is used in the making of ornamental jewels, the flesh of the Abalone is considered a great delicacy in China. Abalones have a wide range and are known by various names—in Australia as Mutton Fish, and in England as Ear Shells. Found along California coastlines, they are protected by law against over-collecting.

ATLANTIC WINGED OYSTER
Pteria colymbus—to 3"
North Carolina to Florida, and West Indies. Shallow water but below low-tide mark.

HOOKED MUSSEL (right)
Brachidontes recurvus—1"-2½"
Atlantic coastline from Cape Cod south to the Caribbean.

CALICO SCALLOP
Aequipecten gibbus—1"-2"
Two specimens showing color variations. North Carolina to Texas.

ZIGZAG SCALLOP
Pecten ziczac—2"
North Carolina to the Caribbean. The upper valve shown here is slightly concave. It fits the convex, rounded lower valve, as a lid fits a bowl.

GLORIOUS SCALLOP
Pecten gloriosus—to 3"
Southwestern Australia. Bivalves are more highly valued when in natural pairs.

LION'S PAW
Lyropecten nodosus—to 6"
Florida and Caribbean. Sponge divers and shrimp fishermen find beautiful specimens of this showy Scallop in offshore waters.

PACIFIC THORNY OYSTER (open)
Spondylus princeps—5"
Gulf of California.

THORNY OYSTER (closed)
Spondylus americanus—4"

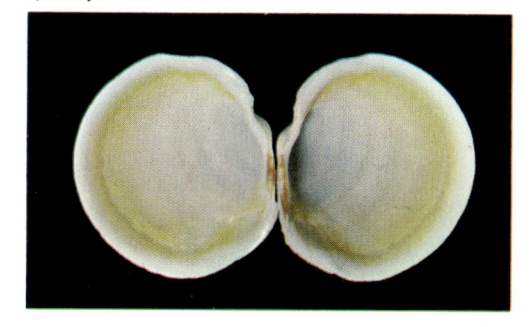

BUTTERCUP LUCINA (right)
Anodontia alba
(formerly *Loripinus chrysostoma*)
$1\frac{1}{2}$"-2". North Carolina to Texas.

CALICO or CHECKERBOARD CLAM (below)
Macrocallista maculata—$2\frac{1}{2}$"
North Carolina to Caribbean. This Clam lives in sand below low-water mark. Albino and dark brown specimens are sometimes found.

PRICKLY or SPINY PAPER COCKLE (below)
Trachycardium egmontianum—2"
North Carolina to Florida.

63

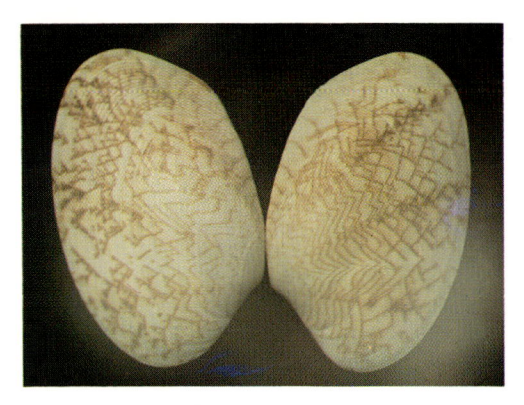

LETTERED VENUS
Tapes literata—3"
Indo-Pacific.

SUNRAY VENUS
Macrocallista nimbosa—to 5"
North Carolina to Texas. Common in Florida, in sandy bays. Prefers shallow water.

FRILLED VENUS (left)
Venus species from Spain's Mediterranean coast—1"
The brown dapples on this beige shell serve as camouflage, blending it into the sand in which the animal lives. Venus Clams have established themselves all over the world.

TELLIN species (above) from the Mediterranean (Malaga, Spain)—kin to the Rose Petal Tellin.

ROSE PETAL TELLIN
Tellina lineata —1½" or less
These pretty Tellins are common in muddy bays. Florida and Caribbean.

box will help you decide whether an object on the bottom is worth diving for. A face mask helps once you are under water.

Storms are the ill winds that blow shell collectors good. After a hurricane the beaches are littered with choice shells, some of them rare species from deep water, that have been blown ashore. Once, in a cove on the Florida Keys, we found tons and tons of dead seaweed and other debris that had been thrown high above the beach by one of these big winds. Cradled among the wrack lay exquisite, perfect Janthinas. As a general rule, the worse the weather the better the shelling!

Some coastlines are incredibly rich in shells. Sanibel Island, on the west coast of Florida near Fort Myers, has been famous among conchologists for years. It is hard to see the sand for the shells, here; there are drifts of shells 3 feet deep, extending the length of the Gulf side of the island. I found more species of shells at Clearwater, Florida, than at Sanibel, though I have never seen Clearwater recommended in a shell collector's handbook. At Clearwater the shells do not cover the beach in drifts and heaps and piles as they do at Sanibel: instead they are deposited individually on the sand as if laid out in a jeweler's window for one to pick and choose. We found the delicate Tusk Shells there, the Winged Oysters (*Pteria*) with linings of lavender and pink and silver, and pairs of Yellow and Rose Tellins. Sanibel has varieties which we did not find at Clearwater, and vice versa. St. Petersburg and the Ten Thousand Islands are recommended by many collectors. In Europe, the Algarve coast of Portugal and the Costa del Sol of Spain are worth a visit. Their climate compares with Florida's. In the Pacific, the Philippine Islands are a shell collector's heaven. Beautiful specimens can be found in Australian waters. Many fine deep-water shells are taken off the coasts of Japan.

The Florida Keys are rich in shells, though not Key West, which has been so built upon that there are few public beaches left. The Middle Keys, however, are worth a trip. We have collected shells in surprising variety on Key Vaca.

On all the beaches you will notice that most of the shells are heavy white Bivalves with horny outer coverings, members of the Ark family. There are more Ark shells on American beaches than shells of all other species put together! There are tremendous numbers of miniature shells, too, but collectors rarely notice these because they are so small. Go through a drift of shells and small debris one day with a magnifying glass, and you may add some unusual little specimens to your collection.

You will probably also add a few fossilized shells to your display as the years go by. Fossils can be found in the most unlikely places; I have picked up a 400,000,000-year-old Brachiopod from the gravel in front of a drive-in restaurant in Kentucky, and a friend collected a fossil Clam from the road bed at Naples, Florida. Brachiopods look like modern seashells, and there are in fact some species of Brachiopods to be found in the ocean today, though they are rare; but they do not belong to the phylum Mollusca. The ancient Brachiopods lived side by side with the ancestors of modern mollusks, but they did not spring from the same stock (so far as can be determined now). Their body plans are dissimilar from those of mollusks.

Many of the Snails that live on land are quite beautiful; the delicate rose-pink *Euglandina Rosea Bullata Gould* (so little known that it has no popular name, though it is very common) can be found in many parts of the southern United States, while the Garden Snails, like the yellow and brown Banded Snails of Europe, deserve a place in any collection. Look in your own back yard at night with a flashlight, for many species are nocturnal, and you may be surprised at what you find! Snails live everywhere; we have found them in woods on the slopes of Alpine mountains, and in cracks in the old stone walls of Agamemnon's city, Mycenae.

The finest shells are usually found on living mollusks; and though very few species have any legal protection against shell hunters, the vast majority of collectors see no reason to kill unnecessarily and take only those they really want.

It is a good idea to sit down at the end of each shelling trip and sort out your shells. You will almost certainly find you have duplicates in your bag, and specimens that are not worth the trouble of carrying home and cleaning. Now is the time to put back those you do not intend to keep for your collection or for trading with other collectors. One or two specimens of each species are all you will need in your own collection, unless of course there are great varieties of form or coloring within a species which you would like to display. If you make a pig of yourself you will only collect a lot of shells you have no use for, to take up storage room!

Cleaning and Displaying Shells

Finding and displaying lovely shells is fun; but before they can be displayed they must be cleaned. Often the specimens you bring home will be muddy, or have their beauty hidden under a coat of green algae. Those taken alive must be cleaned at once, for shellfish decay rapidly. Don't postpone this chore or your catch will probably end up in the garbage, for the stench of rotten shellfish at close quarters is unendurable.

The best place to clean shells is the kitchen sink, as running water is a necessity. You will need an old toothbrush, a saucepan, a can of scouring powder, and a little detergent. A pair of tweezers and a crochet hook will also be useful, though toothpicks can substitute for these.

Shells that have been washed by the surf and dried in the sun until there are no traces of their builders left inside need little cleaning. Soap and water or a little scouring powder will take off any mud or algae the waves have left. Sometimes these "dead" shells are encrusted with barnacles, which can be removed by soaking the shells in water for a few hours and then tapping the barnacles sideways, quite gently, with a knife handle. If one is stubborn, place the blunt edge of the knife blade across its top and press down lightly; it will split and come away in pieces. The whitish rings left at the site of the colony can be removed by scratching them away gently with the point of your crochet hook. This treatment would break a fragile shell, but for some reason barnacles prefer to build on strong, chunky foundations. We have never found a barnacle on a delicate shell.

Shells taken alive are more of a problem. Bivalves will open up if you drop them into water which has been boiled and allowed to cool. Boiling removes the oxygen from the water so that mollusks suffocate when placed in it. After a few minutes their adductor muscles will relax, allowing their valves to spring apart. Scoop them out, scrape the meat out with the tweezers, and wash the shells in soapy water. Shells containing hermit crabs get the same treatment; once the crab relaxes its grip on the shell it can be eased out with tweezers. Be gentle or the end of the tail will break off and remain hooked to the core of the shell, out of reach.

There are several methods of cleaning Univalves taken alive. The procedure least likely to damage their shells is very simple: leave them to soak in water, out of doors, until they rot and come out in bits. The water must be changed daily, or the acids from the rotting meat will accumulate and pit the shells. After the soft parts have disintegrated, a thorough rinsing is needed to make the shells sweet-smelling and fit to come indoors. To avoid getting operculums mixed up, put similar-sized shells in separate containers. Be sure your specimens are out of reach of dogs, cats, and children while they are soaking! This method of cleaning is called "spoiling out"; but it is rather smelly and unpleasant.

Some collectors clean large shells by putting them in ant heaps and letting the ants do the work! If you try this, remove the operculum first, and number it and the shell with ink, so you can unite them again. Ants do a thorough cleaning job, but they pull small shells down into their nests and separate them from their trapdoors. Once small specimens are buried it is hard to find them again, so this lazy way of cleaning them is rather risky.

Perhaps the best way is to put your shells in a pan of warm water and bring it to a boil. Remember, though, that sudden changes in temperature will crack and spoil the surface of glossy shells like Olives and Cowries; when cleaning this type of shell the water must be heated very slowly and allowed to cool gradually.

The length of time the shells must be boiled depends on their size. Err on the side of too much boiling rather than too little; large specimens may take half an hour. When they have cooled to the touch take them from the water one at a time and ease the meat out with a crochet hook. Insert the hook at the siphonal canal and work it well up into the flesh before you start to pull it out, turning the shell as you pull, to gently "unscrew" the dead mollusk. As the flesh cools it shrinks, pulling away from the walls of its home, so it is easy to pull out; but as it shrinks it also retracts from the aperture, making it harder to reach with the hook. If you wait until it is quite cold you may not be able to see the flesh through the aperture at all. Sometimes, however careful you are, the meat will break off deep within the shell and it will be necessary to spoil out the piece left behind.

Snails with only a few whorls will come out easily if you freeze them and then let them thaw slowly. The meat shrinks away from the shell under this treatment. Many spiraled shells, though, cannot be cleaned in this way, as the meat shrinks back out of reach into the upper spirals.

If a delicate specimen needs algae and dirt removed, it is wise to clean it before removing meat, as the animal's solid flesh supports the shell and makes it less likely to break. When handling frail shells be careful to avoid pressure on the lip, which has little structural support and will crumble almost at a touch. It is safest to spoil out these shells. Tiny specimens can simply be left exposed to the air in a covered pan, far away from the house and out of reach of animals, until all objectionable odors are gone; then a few hours soaking in a pan of alcohol will make them fit for display.

Alcohol dries out the shell as well as the flesh within, so rinse your shells thoroughly to remove it or it may dull their finish. A 70 per cent alcohol solution will preserve a mollusk's soft body if you wish to keep it for study; needless to say, the flesh will spoil unless it is kept in its alcohol bath.

If you ever forget to clean a shell for several days after collecting it, don't attempt the task. Let it sit well away from the house for a couple of months, until Nature has taken care of the matter. We once tried to clean some Thais shells two weeks after collecting them; it was a revolting experience! Cleaning live shells sometimes poses a problem; if you are staying in a motel without kitchenette while on vacation, for example, you cannot boil water, and the live shells you find will not wait to be cleaned until you get home! It is a good idea to plan for vacation shelling by keeping a small, inexpensive camp stove in the trunk of your car, and taking an old saucepan and your crochet hook along.

Chitons will curl up if they are unbound before cleaning, and their empty shells tend to curl as they dry, so it is best to keep them bound flat as much as possible. Drop them, with the strips of wood they are on, in the boiled water you used for Bivalves and shells containing hermit crabs. Leave them for an hour, unbind them, and scrape out their flesh carefully to avoid damaging the girdle that holds their plates of shell together. Re-tie them to the wood and let them dry thoroughly in this position before adding them to the collection.

Thick deposits of lime or coral on a shell will come off in a 20 per cent or stronger solution of laundry bleach. This solution will fade the colors if shells are left to soak for very long, however. After bleaching, they will need an extra thorough rinsing. Some handbooks suggest using caustic soda or muriatic acid to remove lime deposits. This will certainly brighten the colors of some species, but acid treatment gives a shell an unnatural appearance and ruins it as a specimen. If you want to experiment, remember that acid burns clothing and fingers as well as shell. Use a weak solution to start with, and work on poor or worthless specimens for practice. Apply the solution to a small area at a time with a paint-brush and rinse immediately. Wear rubber gloves and old clothes, hold the shell with tweezers if it is not too large, and stay near the faucet. If you do splash the acid on you, rinse it off as quickly as you can and keep the water running over the skin for several minutes to make sure every molecule is flushed away.

Most collectors leave the epidermis on their shells, feeling that it is a natural part of the mollusk and it would be a mutilation to remove it. Some like to clean it off so they can see more of the sculpture and colors of the shell. Often the epidermis, or periostracum, is quite attractive; the pitchy black "whiskers" of some of the Ark shells are prettier than the plain white shell beneath. In some families, such as Cones, the epidermis is drab and hides the beauty of the glossy patterned shells it covers. We usually leave the periostracum on if it is pretty or unusual, or if there is no reason to remove it. If you plan to keep more than one specimen of each species you might leave one its epidermis, and clean the other specimen off.

Now that your shells are clean, you may notice that some of them are not so pretty as they were when you found them on the beach. Boiling, scrubbing, and soaking in alcohol all tend to make shells look parched and dried out. A thin coat of mineral oil, wiped on gently with a soft rag, will restore their original good looks and also keep the hinges of Bivalves and periostracums of all species from growing brittle over the years.

Your shells are now ready to be displayed. Too often, people do this haphazardly. Don't start out this way. Those who don't arrange their shells usually stop collecting after a while, saying "What's the use of getting any more? I can only show off so many shells, you know." This is quite true if the shells in your display are duplicates. As a general rule you should only display one or two specimens of each species. There are many reasons for breaking this rule, though: you might wish to display 20 pairs of the gaily marked Coquinas to show the range of colors and variety of markings that can be found. Always display only your best specimens, and try to keep the families together. Then, when you show the collection to friends, you can point out the differences between Arks from New England and Florida, and between shells from America and another country halfway round the world. You may wish to specialize in shells of one particular family, Cowries or Tellins, for example. If you wish, you can trade specimens with other collectors, extending the range of your collection. The duplicate shells which are your storage headache will be the pride and joy of a conchologist in Japan or Australia, while his spares will enrich your display.

Some collectors feel that buying shells is unsportsmanlike; this, of course, is a matter of opinion, but it does seem that there is more fun in building up a fine collection by your own efforts than in paying for professional help. Your collection can be anything you care to make it. There are some people who would not pick up the rarest Cone in the world if it were washed up at their feet because they are only interested in fossilized Snails that lived a million years ago. Others want only the prettiest shells, or the oddest shells. Whatever you choose to collect, you should build the collection on orderly lines, grouping your specimens according to species and family, and country of origin.

Every collector wants to know the names of his shells. This book shows color pictures of various shells to get you familiar with their types and colors. As you progress, you will need a really comprehensive identification guide, containing photos of as many different species as possible, to avoid the frustration of trying to match your shell to a poor picture, or worse, the misery of trying to identify a species not pictured at all.

To identify a shell, look through your large identification guide until you find a picture of one similar to yours, and then look up the description of that species in the text. Species within families are listed together, so if you have not found the exact description of your shell look up descriptions of close kin of the shell that most nearly resemble yours; you will probably find your specimen listed there. Remember that specimens vary in size and coloring; the shell photographed may not be an exact match to the one you have. Shells found on the beach are not always seashells, for storms wash mollusks from the swamps and low ground out to sea and cast them up on the shore; so if you find a Univalve which cannot be identified it is worth trying a guide to Land Snails of the area.

From time to time every collector finds a shell he simply cannot identify. Museum shell collections are a help here; every shell in such a collection is labeled and it is usually fairly simple to find the name of your problem shell. If it is not on display, the museum workers may be able to help you to identify it. As a last resort, and only after you have exerted every possible effort to identify the specimen yourself, the staff of the Smithsonian Institution in Washington, D.C. will help you if you send them the shell, with a letter stating when and where it was found. It is a courtesy to send one or two duplicate specimens which they may keep for the Smithsonian's collection in the event that the problem shell turns out to be a new species, or of interest to science in some other way; your note should say whether or not you want the duplicates returned. We have found busy, world-renowned scientists to be most courteous and helpful; but their kindness must not be abused.

Once you have identified your shells, which should be done as soon as they are cleaned, get a notebook or make an index card file and write down where and when they were found. Scientists and collectors alike feel that shells without this information are of little interest, and if you wish to exchange shells with other collectors later on you will find that you cannot remember where they were found; so write it down! My shell catalogue looks like this:

NUMBER	DATE	PLACE FOUND	NAME	REMARKS
405	1 May 1969	Bay side Sanibel Isl. ½ mile from west end	Common Slipper Shell (*Crepidula fornicata*)	Live, on live oyster

The number is assigned to each shell as it is found to avoid mixing up specimens. The first shell entered will be #1, and so on. Put the number on the shell itself, with a fine nibbed pen and India ink, in an inconspicuous place. Make your location entry as accurate and exact as possible. Use of the Latin name is useful when exchanging specimens; it will save you from sending Butterflies and receiving the same shells called Pompanos or Coquinas in exchange (all of them local names for the same shell, *Donax Variabilis*). Under remarks, note who collected the specimens if you did not, and anything unusual or interesting about the find.

Duplicate specimens intended for exchange or gift should be stored in orderly fashion, or it will take you an hour's work to find a particular shell you want in the jumble. Cigar boxes make good storage units for all but the large species; they should be labeled with their contents ("Cones," "Murex," "Janthinas" etc.), to simplify locating what is needed.

Some collectors display their shells in cotton-lined drawers, while others prefer shelves or boxes containing several trays resting on one another. Any sturdy container, a cigar box or an old fishing tackle box, for example, can be used to begin with. Stacks of empty matchboxes, glued together and lined with cotton, provide storage for miniature shells. A coating of adhesive-backed plastic makes such a "chest" more presentable. A metal cabinet with plastic drawers, designed to hold small items, and with a label-holding slot on the front of each drawer is ideal for smaller species. Bivalves can be shown off in flat, velvet-lined butterfly boxes obtainable from museum shops. These boxes, or ordinary flat cardboard boxes with clear acetate tops, are handy for exhibiting shells as they keep dust and curious fingers out.

A few of your choicest specimens can grace the shelves of a room divider in your living room, or be displayed in a recess under a glass-topped coffee table. Artificial light will not damage shells, but strong sunlight will fade them in time, so don't put them on a window sill unless they are easily replaceable. Don't be so afraid of harm coming to them, though, that you keep them forever hidden in cotton-packed boxes. Like all lovely things, they deserve to be seen and admired.

This fossil Clam was found in a road bed in Golden Gates, Florida. Fossil shells, which may be many thousands of years old, are fun to collect and compare with modern shells.

4 Man and Mollusk

Shells in Prehistory

AGES AGO a primitive human being first foraged a beach and satisfied his hunger with raw shellfish. Since that day people have used mollusks, originally for food, and later for commercial and aesthetic purposes. The story of man and mollusk is absorbing, though its earliest chapters are irretrievably lost. In those days lore and legend were passed down from generation to generation by word of mouth, becoming blurred and forgotten with time. Shells, however, are concrete things, not easily destroyed; they afford clear evidence of prehistoric events to those who can read the tale they have to tell. Much of the story has been uncovered by archeologists, and every few years they make a discovery that helps to fill in its gaps.

For instance, such a discovery took place when some workers building a railway line in France, in 1867, uncovered the remains of five people. Among the bones lay shell ornaments. Archeologists from all over the world came to study the find. They concluded that the bones were those of people who had lived in the area some 30,000 years before, members of a tall, slender race called Cro-Magnon. The little group—three men, a woman, and a child in the group—had been murdered. Apparently robbery was not the motive, for weapons, tools, elaborate ornaments of animal's teeth, and seashell necklaces were found along with the bones.

The archeologists who came to look at this find stayed on to dig in the area, and uncovered several other Cro-Magnon burial places. The dead had been treated with respect and ceremony: the bodies were coated with red ochre, and the weapons and ornaments they used in life lay beside them. The most interesting thing is that these graves, far inland, contained seashell necklaces. It is reasonable to think that the necklaces were made by people who lived near the sea, and then traded to other tribes; they may have changed hands repeatedly on their journey inland before being bartered to Cro-Magnon people.

Far later in prehistory, about 5,000 years before the birth of Christ, shellfish became a staple food. At this time agriculture was unknown in Europe, and the people lived a nomadic life as hunters. When game was plentiful they glutted themselves, and when it was scarce they starved. Then someone realized that the Oyster beds on the coastlines of northern Europe could support a more settled form of existence. People could build better, warmer houses, accumulate more possessions, and generally have a happier life if they were not always moving from place to place. The idea spread and tribes settled down to village life. They still obtained most of their food by hunting, but now they had Oysters and other shellfish to fall back on when the deer evaded their flint-tipped arrows. They were called "Kitchen-Midden People" because the sites of their villages are marked by enormous communal garbage dumps (middens) of empty shells and bones. As the centuries passed they became expert fishermen and skilled flint-workers.

Later on, in the Stone Age, colonists began to trickle in from the east, bringing with them a knowledge of agriculture; their skills, combined with those of the fisherfolk, brought a sudden improvement in the standard of living. These people also used shells for ornamental purposes, and some of the shells came from far away. Cowries from the Red Sea and Indian Ocean have been found with their bodies, entombed in the cold earth of northern Europe. Traders did not barter these shells across two continents for nothing; high prices must have been paid to induce men to carry the tropical Cowries so far. How many times did a shell change hands before adorning the neck of a Scandinavian princess? The journey must have taken years—across deserts by camel-caravan and the Mediterranean aboard a galley rowed by slaves, then across the sun-parched plains of Italy and over the Alps on the back of a mule.

The next advance in man's use of mollusks came a thousand years later. Much of our knowledge of life in this period is drawn from the Bible, both directly and indirectly; for archeologists deduced the sites of forgotten cities from accounts in the Old Testament and put theory into practice by digging them up! One of these cities, mentioned in the Bible as the home of Abraham, was the fabled Ur of the Chaldees.

Today the streets of Ur are ruined and empty; but long ago, when the Sumerians lived there, they were full of busy people going about their daily tasks. These people, living in fine houses in an age of luxury, made elaborate preparations to continue to live the same way after death—for they believed they would live on in a spirit world. The worldly possessions which mourners felt a dead personage might need were placed around him: food, chariot, harp, ornaments, and precious metals. We owe to these customs a vast store of knowledge about the lives of wealthy people of the times; sealed in hidden tombs, the record of their civilization came down to us intact.

Shells were highly valued for their beauty during this period. When the royal tombs at Ur were discovered, the remains of Sumerian queens were found, decked in headdresses of gold inlaid with shell and lapis lazuli. Sumerian lapidaries were famous for their inlay work; the tombs yielded a rich treasure of golden jewels, sculptures, ladies' dressing boxes and gentlemen's gaming boards, all inlaid with the carved mother-of-pearl shell and lapis lazuli they liked so well. Even today, nearly 5,000 years after they were made, the colors are still fresh and bright.

The settlers who came to the Euphrates valley imported new religions. Statues of their gods were set up everywhere; finely executed by the standards of the day, they were made to look as lifelike as possible with stains and inlay work. Eyeballs were cut from white shell, irises from dark stone. Carefully carved hair was stained dark with bitumen.

In the last couple of centuries people have learned so much about dyes and dye-making that now you can buy fabric in any shade or color you desire. In the ancient world, however, only a few coloring agents were known; these were obtained by boiling plants and roots and were so highly diluted that it was impossible to produce deep, rich colors. Dyers tried to copy the gorgeous hues of roses and violets, but without success. Then one day someone found that Murex species common in the Mediterranean squirt ink to form a smoke screen when alarmed, and that the ink would color fabric steeped in it a rich purple. Tradition says the first dye was made from Murex ink at the famous Phoenician seaport of Tyre; at all events, an industry sprang up there that was to make "Tyrian purple" a household word around the Mediterranean. The word "purple" comes from *purpura*, one of three species of Murex that the Tyrians processed into dye.

As word of the discovery spread, a great demand arose; suddenly every woman wanted a purple silk gown, and unfortunate husbands had to pay fantastic bills to keep their womenfolk up with the "Joneses" of the day. At one time, prices of purple-dyed cloth soared to $12,000 a pound. Phoenician vessels traversed the seas in search of new markets, colonizing far-off lands and spreading their culture in the process. (The Phoenicians had invented the alphabet.) The huge prices they got for the dye were not unreasonable, for a great deal of time and effort went into its preparation. First the Tyrian peasants had to gather and crush thousands of Murex shells. The crushed mollusks were put in great kettles, with water and a little salt, and boiled for days to extract their ink. Then the boiled-down liquid was allowed to stand. Each boiling yielded only a small amount of the precious substance, so it was no wonder it was highly valued. Slowly it turned

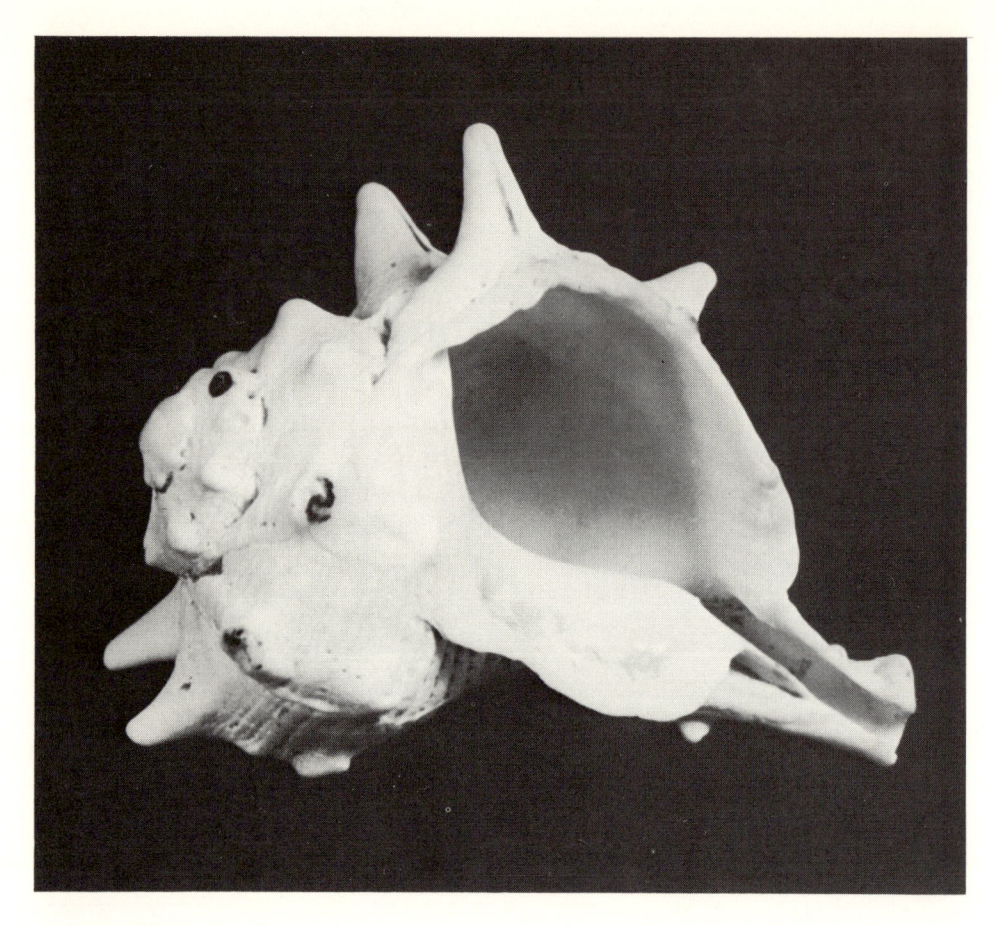

DYE MUREX
Murex brandaris—3"
Expressions such as "red carpet" and "born to the purple" sprung from the famous purple dye derived from the ink of the Murex. Treasured in early times by kings and queens, the dye caused the Phoenician city, Tyre, to become the hub of an important industry. The extraction of the ink and the manufacturing of purple cloth made Tyre a household word throughout the ancient world. The Murex' ink is a defense mechanism—released into the water as a smoke screen it allows its owner to escape from enemies. Before its discovery, the closest color to purple was a soft mauve, produced from herbs and tree barks.

yellow, then green, then blue, and finally a purple or rich scarlet. When we say purple we know exactly what color we mean; the ancients were not so sure. In those days purple meant any color from indigo to deep crimson! Knowing that purple could mean crimson, it is easy for us to see why Roman ladies used Tyrian dye as a cosmetic, staining lips and cheeks to a rosy glow.

Throughout the ages, people have sought the most rare and precious appointments for their temples; according to the Old Testament, Moses was directed to prepare a Sanctuary for the Ark of the Covenant, and cloths of Tyrian purple were considered worthy for this purpose. The curtains of the Sanctuary were to be "of fine linen, violet, purple, and scarlet" (*Exodus*, v26–39). The priests of the Sanctuary were to be robed in the same hue, with trimmings and fastenings of gold.

The Tyrians were getting rich; but setbacks were to come. The Emperor of Rome annexed purple as *his* imperial color. From then on, "wearers of the purple" were to be Romans of royal blood and high rank only, for no one else was allowed to use the dye. Of course, the laws were sidestepped as time went by, as unpopular laws usually are; but even today we think of purple as a regal, proud color; kings wear purple at their coronations, crimson carpets are laid for visiting dignitaries, and purple velvet hangings lend an air of austere, formal elegance to the reception rooms of palaces.

Today, the coins of ancient Tyre with their murex design are no longer used in commerce. Modern chemistry has made purple available inexpensively to all. But some native races, such as Mexico's Tehuantepec Indians, still use dyes from mollusks to tint their cotton goods.

During the Middle Ages a shell came to be the symbol of pilgrimage. About 1000 A.D., European pilgrims frequently banded together to visit the Holy Land, which was under Mohammedan rule. These pilgrimages had taken place peaceably enough for centuries, but then the church in Europe felt the temper of the times, saw an opportunity to regain control of the Holy Land, and called for a Holy War. The Crusades began.

Soon thousands of armed men arrived in Syria. They strolled along the sun-drenched beaches, which were strewn with valves of a pretty, gaily-colored Scallop common in the area. The shells were novelties, so they were picked up and saved. Many of the men took them home after the Crusades as curiosities to show their wives. As time went by, the valves became cherished mementoes, kept and displayed by families as proof that their menfolk had made the long, dangerous journey to Jerusalem, and perhaps even fought the Saracen. When the king knighted some of these men for services to their country it was only natural that they should choose to include the Scallop shell, their badge of honor, among the

77

emblems on their coats-of-arms. This is why, today, many of England's leading families bear on their crests the outline of a common seashell.

Many a Crusader returning from the East brought home an unusual gift—a pair of gloves so fine that they could fit into a walnut shell. These gloves were made of the byssus which Pinnas (bivalves with large, horny, triangular shells) spin to attach themselves to sandy bottoms. This byssus was gathered and woven, alone or blended with silk, into the ancients' "cloth of gold." Historians believe that Jason's Golden Fleece may actually have been this rare and valuable fabric. Pinnas are common in many parts of the world; they litter the beaches of Florida's Sanibel Island so thickly that you cannot avoid stepping on them.

Food and ornament, dyes and cosmetics and manufactured goods . . . the people of the Old World found mollusks very useful. But what part did they play in the history of the New World? How did the first Americans use shells?

The men and women who colonized the Americas lived and died thousands of years before Eric the Red saw Vinland. They had no written language, so all we know of them is what we can learn from their remains and artifacts. We do not even know when the first child was born in America. Scientists believe that man originated in Africa, and no one lived in America when Java Man or Peking Man trod the earth of the Old World. Just how and when he arrived in America we are not sure. Some authorities believe he came from Scandinavia, following the sea routes that the Vikings took later on; some think he crossed the Pacific to the western shores of South America. There is evidence that people did come by these routes, but the consensus of opinion now is that almost all of the first Americans came across the Bering Strait from Asia. It is known that about 20,000 years ago, when the last Ice Age was easing its grip on the world, this 125-foot-deep Strait was either frozen over or else dry land, linking Siberia to Alaska with a bridge. At this time the crossing would have been fairly easy.

Many groups of people, hoping for better hunting, must have made the trek, landing in Alaska with their families and dogs. But some were still dissatisfied, for the new country was as cold and inhospitable as the one they had left. They moved south to milder climates and easier living.

In a paradise of unsuspecting game and shorter winters they settled down to enjoy life. Their death rate fell sharply, and soon tribes found they had too many members; they were overhunting the territory in which they had settled. Groups split, going in search of fresh hunting grounds. The frontiers of man were pushed back very slowly, but at last, after 12,000 years, every part of the Americas was colonized. Distance and lack of communication made invisible walls between tribes, fostering the development of varied dialects, languages, and cultures.

Not too long after the country which was to be Minnesota was settled, a young girl drowned in the icy waters of a glacial lake. Years and centuries went by and became thousands of years; Columbus set sail, America declared its independence, and Minnesota became a state. Roads were carved across the wilderness, and in their building the bones of the Ice Age girl were found. She had carried a knife of elkhorn at her side, strung on a thong through a neatly pierced hole at the handle end. Around her neck she had worn a conch shell from waters far to the south—evidence that "interstate commerce" had already begun! Authorities studied her fossilized remains and the things she had worn on her fatal swim; students dubbed her Minnesota Minnie. Her accidental discovery by road workers caused American archeologists to dig with added zeal. As they delved, they added scrap after scrap of information to our store of knowledge of the lives of early Americans. Some of these discoveries concerned their use of seashells.

Many tribes of American Indians were lovers of beauty. They liked to make necessities attractive, carving and painting their houses and canoes, and weaving beautiful patterns into their blankets and clothing. They learned to get dyes from plants and barks, and discovered the purple of the Murex and Thais shells. They wove bird feathers into fabric to make warm coverings. Their pottery was highly decorated, and their wooden dishes were carved and inlaid with shell. Some tribes used Dentalium or tooth shells for money, stringing them together by passing a thread through the length of each shell. Other tribes used the famous shell coinage, wampum. Wampum was made of tubular beads ground out of the shell of a common Clam which we call by its Indian name, Quahog. The valves are mostly white, but there is a purple splotch on the inside, near the rim. Only a few purple beads could be obtained from each shell, so purple wampum was valued more highly than white.

The Indians who lived near the sea were not financial tycoons with their own private mint, however. First they had to collect the shells and chip out the rough beads. Then each bead had to be filed down and smoothed by hand—a long, tedious process. Once smoothed, the final step was the drilling of the hole with a sliver of extremely hard material, such as bone or flint. Each finished bead represented hours of work, and thus had a high intrinsic value. It is said that white traders tried to make their own wampum, found out how much work was involved, and gave up in disgust.

The Indians used to keep records of important events by weaving meaningful patterns into belts of wampum beads. In general, white designs indicated peaceful events, with purple showing death or war. Each collection of belt records had a keeper, an Indian historian who was versed in the sign language used and could interpret the events recorded on old belts long after those who made them had died and been forgotten.

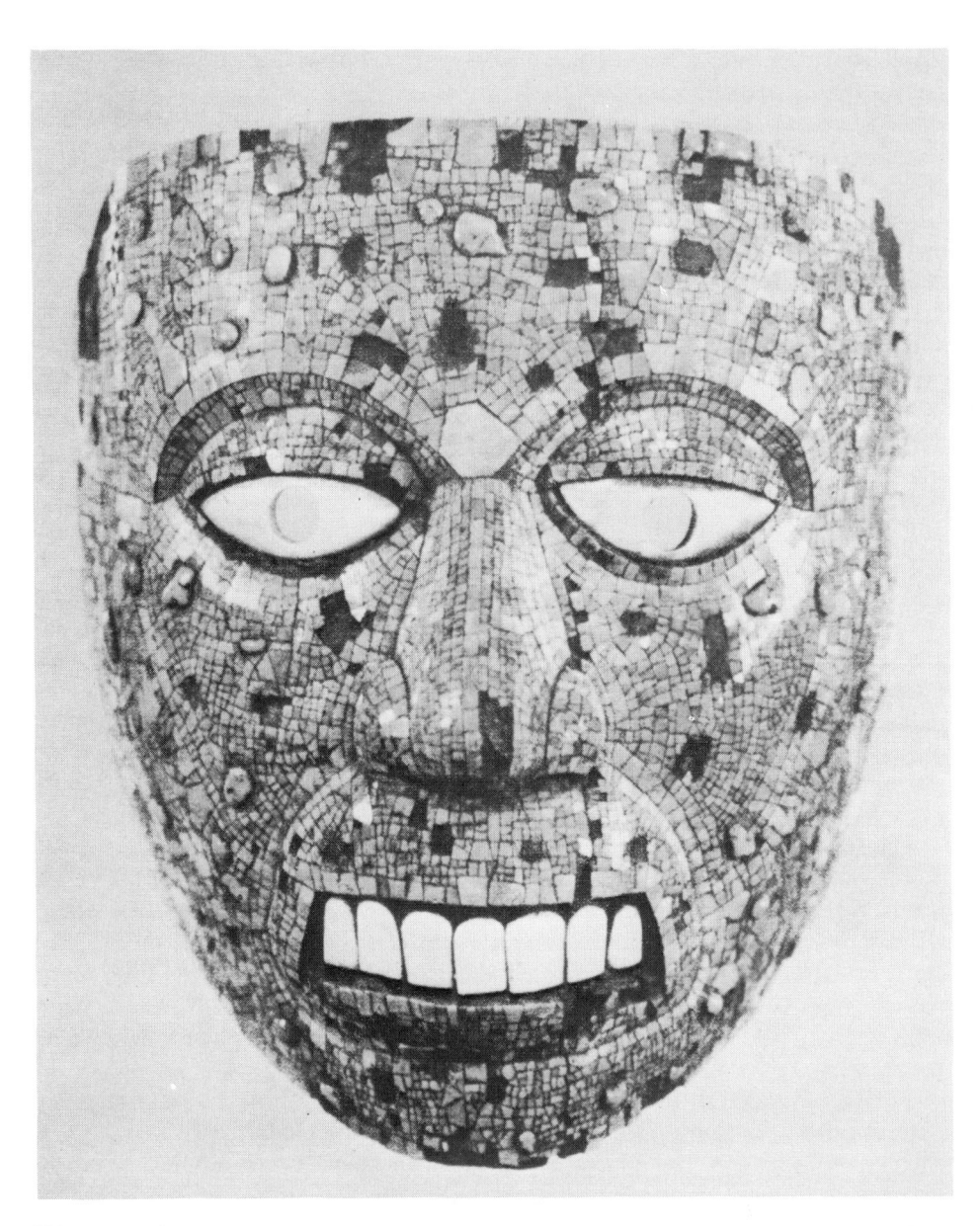

This ceremonial mask, once used in Aztec sacrificial rites, is a turquoise and shell mosaic. From Mexico, it represents the Aztec god, Quetzalcoatl. Its eyes and teeth are of white shell.

Like the Kitchen-Midden people of Europe, the Indians were fond of shellfish. Women dug Clams with sticks, stewing part of their catch to eat at once and smoking the rest for future use. They smoked the Clams by taking them from the shells and stringing them on sticks like kabobs, propping them in the smoke of a slow fire until the flesh was thoroughly cured.

Further south in the Americas two great civilizations were flowering—the Aztec in Mexico and the Inca in Peru. By our standards the Aztecs were a barbarous people, living in luxury, building great pyramids, adorning themselves with golden ornaments, yet practicing human sacrifice and ritual cannibalism. They believed that their God must have human blood in order to live, and they kept him amply provided with that sustenance. Great numbers of sacrificial victims (20,000 were reported to have died at one festival, just before the Spanish arrived) were spread-eagled on the altars atop the pyramids to have their hearts cut from their living bodies. Offerings of gold and mosaics of turquoise and shell were thrown into sacrificial wells to appease the rain gods. Women and children were also thrown in.

When the Spanish Conquistadors came to America they heard of the wealth of the Aztec nation, and destroyed the Aztecs to get it. The Aztec emperor, Montezuma, was taken prisoner. After the Spaniards burned a half dozen Aztec nobles alive, Montezuma ordered his people to give their captors the gold they demanded. About $6,000,000 worth of gold jewelry, ornaments, and statues were brought in and melted into bars for shipment to Spain; but then the Spanish leader, Cortez, made a mistake. The Aztecs were a deeply religious people, and Cortez looted the temples, destroying statues of Aztec gods. The common people rose in fury, drove him from the country, and killed three-fourths of his men. Those they captured were sacrificed in the temples they had profaned. Cortez, however, collected another army and attacked again. This time he conquered them completely, regained his stolen treasure, and imposed Spanish government and religion on the remnants of the proud people.

Though Cortez melted down most of the art objects he took, some of them were sent to Spain as curiosities. These have found their way into museums, both in Europe and in the New World. There is an outstanding collection of Aztec art in the British Museum, in London. Among this collection are a number of mosaic ornaments of jade and shell, or turquoise and shell. A ceremonial mask which a priest may have worn at human sacrifices is there, made of turquoise pieces inlaid into a cedarwood base. Its eyes and teeth are of white shell. In the center of each eye is a round hole representing the iris, through which the priest could see. It is a beautiful piece of work, but its expression is cruel and grim.

The Incas, in the remote fastnesses of the Andes Mountains, were a gentler people than the Aztecs, and their religious beliefs did not inspire them to wholesale barbarity. They had an elaborate caste system, in which social rank determined the clothing people were allowed to wear. The richest ornaments might only be worn by the highest nobles. Of all ornaments, the most important were giant earplugs (some, 4 inches across), and worn by men, not women. Teenage boys had their ears pierced with a gold dagger, sometimes by the Inca emperor himself in a coming-of-age ceremony. A small plug was inserted in the hole, pulling the lobe down by its weight and stretching it until it could take an ornament one size larger. Finally, when the man could wear the huge earplugs that denoted his high rank, they hung down almost to his shoulders. The plugs were made of gold, inlaid with figures of turquoise and colored shell mosaic on a background of white shell. Some of them are quite beautiful; but they must have been very heavy and uncomfortable. Although the Aztecs and the Incas were rich in precious metals and semi-precious stones, they still valued seashells for their beauty.

Shells of the South Seas

Half a world away, in the mineral-poor islands of the South Seas, shells were even more highly valued. The most beautiful shells in the world come from the waters that lap these islands; shell lore and legend are woven into the annals of the Pacific.

A thousand miles to the east of Australia is a group of islands called the New Hebrides. A few generations ago headhunting raids and cannibalism were routine events here. Some tribes in the New Hebrides use shell money, obtained in trade from the natives of one particular island, Matanavat, who specialize in its manufacture. The beads are ground from shells by the same process the American Indians used, and the amount of work involved keeps the market from being flooded with shell money. White traders accept this "cash" in barter, knowing that on many Pacific islands it is more readily accepted than silver coins. Suitors thread the beads into necklaces for their betrothed; island women consider it a high privilege to wear such a strand, which has an aesthetic as well as a monetary value (like a diamond necklace!).

These tribes have a complicated social scale which young men must climb. After years of work a man attains a higher status in the community and has certain new privileges. One of these is the right to wear an armlet of shell beads. Made of money beads, threaded and woven into intricate designs, the armlet patterns further indicate the wearer's rank. The parallel between the shell money and patterned armlets of the Pacific and the wampum and record belts of the American Indians is obvious. It is one of the many similarities between the two

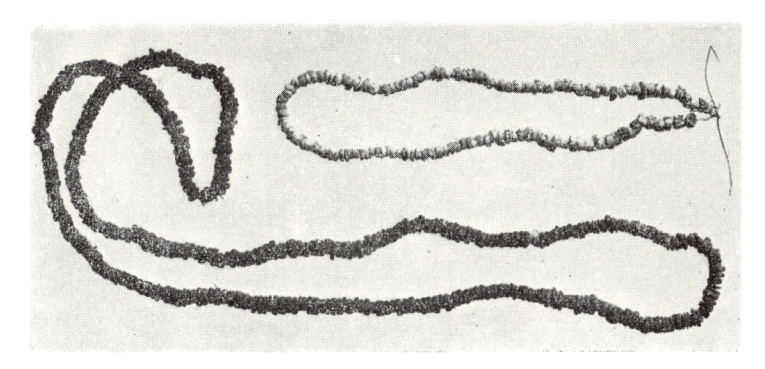

Shells have traditionally been used as currency in the South Seas. These old strings of shell-bead money are from the Solomon Islands. Such shell necklaces, armlets, and bracelets are more highly valued than silver currency.

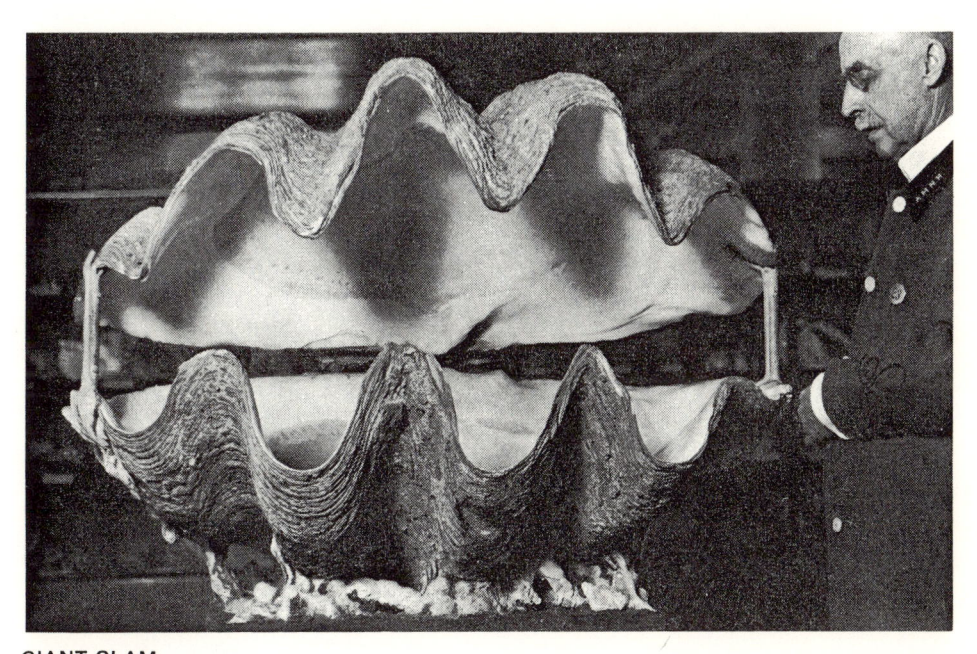

GIANT CLAM
Tridacna gigas—to 4'
The largest Giant Clam shell ever found came from South Pacific waters. It weighs $579\frac{1}{2}$ pounds and measures 43 inches by 29 inches. The Giant Clams provide a tasty meal for the island natives who must be highly skilled at prying the valves apart in the water. A mistake could result in serious injuries, or even death.

cultures that have led anthropologists to speculate that, long ago, islanders may have drifted to America across the Pacific in canoes, or vice versa, so that there was an exchange of customs between the Indians living in the Americas and the Polynesians and Indonesians.

There is a legend in the Pacific, the equivalent of our story of Adam and Eve. It goes something like this:

Once upon a time there was a Giant Clam on the reef of Malekula Island. One day the Clam died, and at the next low tide the first woman came into being by magic, inside its shell. There she lit the first fire. Far away on the island, sitting in a nest high up in the treetops, a tiny bird was singing. He saw the smoke, and flew out to the reef to see what it could be. The smoke poured out from between the valves of the Clam shell, and the bird tried to cut through its hinge with his beak so he could see inside. As he pecked, he grew bigger and bigger, and turned into a man. When he cut through the hinge he was surprised to see the first woman push back the top valve and climb from the shell. They went back to the island together and were married. One day they had a son, who became the first chief of Malekula; and they all lived happily ever after, as people should in legends.

Giant Clams (*Tridacna gigas*) are common in these tropical waters, where they grow up to 5 feet long and weigh as much as 500 pounds, so it is not surprising that they appear in many island legends. Like a number of other shells, Giant Clams have unattractive exteriors. Their heavy valves are covered with coral growths, and are of a dirty white color, but their linings are ivory white and porcelain smooth. You must have seen a single valve used as the basin for an ornamental fountain, or as the font in a church. The coral-encrusted shell holds a living creature of great beauty. Photographs taken underwater show that these Clams have brilliant, many-hued mantles; green mantles, blue mantles, even purple mantles, all splotched and marked with subtle color variations. What purpose this beauty serves is not known. It is certainly no camouflage.

Large as they are, the Clams live on minute animals and plants strained from the water, just as other Bivalves do. Tiny plants have formed an interesting partnership with them: the plants embed themselves in the mantle tissue, where they thrive in the carbon-dioxide-saturated water which the Clam gives off, and in turn emit oxygen which benefits their host. The flesh of the great Clams is good to eat. Natives kick the valves to make them close and then break away the lip of the shell with a stone. Once a hole is made, they thrust in a knife and slice through the adductor muscle to open the Clam. There is a reason for this cautious approach: if a shellfish hunter gets his arm or leg caught between the closing valves he will be badly mangled. If the accident happens underwater, or if he is trapped far out on the reef and no one sees his plight before the tide rises, he will drown.

The natives of a chain of islands near New Guinea could give horsetraders lessons. These men will "give" a friend (or enemy) a particularly fine shell bangle or necklace. The recipient must repay this gift with an equally fine one within a certain length of time, or lose face in the tribe. The ornaments are hard to get, so they are valuable. A bracelet is made from one particular variety of Cone shell which has the spire and narrow whorls filed away to leave only the exterior ring. The larger the ring the more valuable the bracelet, for large shells are uncommon. An especially fine bangle may be a family heirloom, passed down from father to son for generations. The necklaces are discs of red Spondylus shell or mother-of-pearl, polished to a high gloss and worn threaded on thongs. A man who is given such a trinket may be unable to repay it, for he cannot give it back. If he cannot afford to give an equally fine one, he has one way of avoiding disgrace: he can hand the man who put him on the spot a smaller necklace or bangle every few months, until he is in a position to settle the debt with a satisfactory ornament. In the meantime he can always give his present to someone else and perhaps recoup his losses.

In the Solomons, headhunters inlay their great war canoes with mother-of-pearl and Cowrie shells; these canoes are huge things, built of planks cut by hand, each plank from a single tree. The largest war canoes can carry a hundred men. Shells find another use on islands where natives pride themselves on being clean shaven; lacking razors, the men pull unwanted hairs out one by one, using the valves of a small Clam for tweezers.

Perhaps more has been written about the Cowrie than any other seashell. Many people have heard of Cowrie money, and almost everyone knows what the shell looks like—smooth, shiny, egg-shaped, with a slitlike aperture and splotched with color. The Golden Cowrie is unusual in that it is one solid color, a dull gold, without pattern or marking. This rare and beautiful shell is the crown jewel of the chieftains of Fiji Island. Just as a Roman Emperor once annexed Tyrian purple as his royal color, long ago a Fiji chief made the Golden Cowrie his symbol of royalty; and so it remains today. The "money Cowrie" is no longer used as currency, though at one time it was used widely, among the islands and far to the north in Africa. It is a smallish yellow shell, about an inch long; it may be smooth or knobby, and sometimes has a raised ring decorating its upper surface.

Many World War II veterans brought home "cat's eyes" as souvenirs of the Pacific to be made into rings or cuff links. While these are not shells, they are the opercula of Turban Snails.

When a serviceman stationed in the Philippine Islands walks along a beach he has a chance of finding a $3,000 shell—the spotted white-toothed Leucodon Cowrie. This Cowrie is the most valuable shell in the world, for it is extremely rare. Only three are known to exist. Another precious shell is the beautiful Gloria-Maris, the Glory of the Seas Cone. About 4 inches long with orange markings, this large Cone has sold at $2,000 and been valued as high as $3,000. Once the Glory of the Seas was thought extinct, because a volcanic eruption destroyed the reef where the first specimens were found; but in the last few years more have come to light. Today about 70 specimens are known, almost all in museum collections. Collectors and divers in the Philippines are always on the watch for more. It is quite possible that there are Glory of the Seas Cones tucked away in attics, among the shells a father brought home from a war or a great-grandfather collected a century ago.

Many museums display the work of Pacific craftsmen, and shells are much in evidence in these exhibits. Mother-of-pearl eyes decorate effigies of gods carved in dark wood, which once adorned the ridgepoles of meeting houses; mother-of-pearl inlays make beautiful such everyday objects as fishhooks. Small Cones serve as pieces (chips) in Pacific island games. Many of the people who made these things are said to have been savage and cruel, though perhaps no more so than those who exploited them in the name of civilization. Yet their artifacts show that they appreciated beauty, and went to a great deal of trouble to introduce it into their everyday life.

GEOGRAPHY CONE
Conus geographus—5"
This pretty South Pacific Cone has a deadly sting which kills its prey. One Australian specimen took fatal revenge upon its collector by driving its sting into the man's hand. He died within two hours. Although it poisons the meat of its victims, the Cone apparently has a built-in immunity to its own venom, since it kills for food.

5 Mollusks as a Business

Food for a Hungry World

WE LIVE TODAY in an age of plastic beads and paper money; yet mollusks retain their usefulness to man. Empty shells are used for many purposes. In the Mississippi Valley, 700,000,000,000 fresh-water Mussels are put through machines which turn them into mother-of-pearl buttons each year. In Florida, houses are built of blocks of coquina, a building material composed of Coquina shells and coral bound with cement. And along the Gulf Coast, roads are built on Oyster-shell foundations. Many species are valued for their meat.

The seafood industry is big business, and is likely to get bigger, for the world's population is expected to triple by the end of the century and it is already pushing at the limits of its food supply. While most arable land is already being used, only a tiny fraction of the protein-rich food which the seas have to offer us is currently harvested.

Where gourmets gather, Oysters are served. These delectable Bivalves, prized by epicures since Greek and Roman times, are farmed commercially. Millions of Oysters can be harvested from a small undersea acreage, if they are farmed in a suitable environment and proper care is given to the beds. In the United States and other places, laws govern the length of the harvesting season and the size of the Oysters which may be taken; when unusually small numbers are found the season is shortened, to make sure that enough mature Oysters will be left to breed and repopulate the Oyster beds. The beds are patrolled, and in some places radar is used to control out-of-season poaching. One town, Pass Christian, Mississippi, is purchasing a radar system that will scan Oyster beds 12 to 16 miles offshore.

In some states, there are laws requiring oystermen to dump a certain proportion of the shells of the Oysters they take back into the sea, to provide firm surfaces for the young mollusks, called "spat," to settle on. This practice is known as "cultching" the beds. Oysters have a couple of peculiarities shared by few mollusks: they change their sex several times in the course of their lives, and they like to live with a valve of shell above and a valve below their soft bodies; most Bivalves prefer to settle down with a valve on either side vertically.

In France and Japan, Oysters are cultivated on frameworks of poles and tiles, as they have been for centuries. England's Oyster fisheries received a cruel blow about 40 years ago, when a sharp drop in the harvest led to a disastrous attempt to repopulate the Oyster grounds. American spat were imported; but tiny Drills and Slipper Shells came with them. As the young Oysters grew, the growing Drills and Slippers killed them off; mature, the pests bred and multiplied, decimating what was left of the native Oyster population and crossing the Channel to invade the French fisheries. Although the Slipper Shells do not bore holes through the Oyster shells to eat the meat within, as the Drills do, they are just as deadly: they settle down in colonies on top of the Oysters, siphoning off oxygen and suspended food from the water until their unwilling hosts starve and suffocate.

Cockles and Mussels are virtually ignored in America, though they are an important item of food in many countries. The Cockles live in mud, like Clams. Before long, Mussels may become a major source of protein for a hungry world: an acre of good Mussel bed produces up to 10,000 pounds of meat in a year, while an acre of good pasture produces only 200 pounds of beef in the same time. Modern tastes may be geared to steak, but many people find Mussels are delicious. In Spain, Mussels are a major ingredient of the delicious national seafood potpourri, *paella*. Mussels can live in huge colonies because they only need a tiny area to anchor their byssus—the smallest space on a wooden pier will hold a dozen of them. If storms tear them loose or pile mud on them they can move to another site.

In Europe, Scallops are eaten whole, on the half-shell, but in America only the adductor muscle is cooked and served. Clams support a considerable industry; Clam chowder is a specialty dish, particularly in New England, and canned Clam meat and juices are available everywhere. The tiny Coquina Clams are used for chowder, too, making up by abundance what they lack in size. The common East Coast Clam, *Venus mercenaria Linnaeus*, has a dozen or more local names. Halfgrown specimens are called Cherrystones, and mature Clams are sold as Hard Shells, Quahogs, Round Clams, and Little Necks, depending on where they were caught. If you trade Clam shells with another collector without giving the Latin name of your shell first, you may find you have received exactly the same species you sent!

Abalones until recently were very common on California beaches, but now they are scarce, for they were hunted commercially for their flesh, which was dried and exported to China as a delicacy. Tenderized by pounding, the foot is sold and eaten as Abalone steak. The mother-of-pearl lining of the shell is a thing of beauty, frequently used in jewelry making. If you have a chance to visit one of the Mexican cities where every store on Main Street is a souvenir shop, you will see beautiful, inexpensive Abalone shell jewelry. The Mexican workers slice off pieces of lining, carve them into leaves, flower petals, or geometrical shapes for men's jewelry, and set them in silver mountings. This jewelry can be worn with many colors, for the subtle grey of the shell is iridescent with pink and green and lavender and blue; it picks up anything it is placed upon.

Many species of mollusks are edible, although few have attained more than local fame. In England, Periwinkles and Whelks are boiled and sold from barrows on the streets of seaside resorts, as a delicacy; with each bag of Winkles, the purchaser gets a pin to pull the meat from the shells! In France, Escargots (Snails) are savoured by gourmets. They are cooked in a butter and garlic sauce, and served in their shells. These Snails are land dwellers, cultivated on farms for shipment to markets and restaurants all over Europe.

All along the Mediterranean shores, Octopi and small Squids are harvested for food. We spotted them, baked in a tomato sauce, in the cafeteria of a department store in Naples, Italy, and found them surprisingly good, though a little stringy. They are also served as an ingredient of the Italian *zuppa de pesca*, a chowder served as a kind of seafood stew, containing anything and everything edible the fishermen happen to catch. In Japan, Octopi are pickled and served for breakfast or any meal!

Jewels from the Sea

Of all the ornaments which have been taken from the sea to grace fair women, the pearl is queen. It ranks with precious stones for costliness and beauty.

Although the people of the ancient world were well aware of the value and beauty of pearls and knew they were to be found in Oysters, they did not know how pearls were made. Educated men had very fanciful theories and made wild guesses. Pliny the Elder, for instance, one of the most respected and highly educated men of his day, surmised that pearls resulted when dew fell on female Oysters at low tide.

The truth of the matter is not very romantic. A speck of foreign matter such as a grain of sand or a tiny animal gets under the mantle of an Oyster, causing irritation. As the irritant passes through the mantle tissue and enters the mollusk's body it tears off and carries with it a few cells of this tissue. The mantle cells grow and continue to secrete nacre, the material which forms mother-of-pearl and pearls, in their new position. Nacre cells and foreign particles together form what could be called a pearl cyst. If the cyst comes to rest in a cavity of the mollusk's body it can grow into a sphere, for the nacre laid down on the unwanted particle forms at the same rate on all parts of it; this is how a round (or *free*) pearl is formed. If the cyst becomes embedded in muscle, however, its growth in some directions will be retarded, and an irregularly shaped or *baroque* pearl will result. Teardrop-shaped pearls are formed in this way and are very valuable, but most baroque pearls are quite irregular and are of little use. If the cyst lodges between a valve and the mantle, the baroque pearl which results may be attached to the lining of the valve by a thin stalk; these are called *shell* pearls and are also of little value.

Once in a while, a pearl Oyster will form a free pearl, and then build a dome of pearl material over it, imprisoning the pearl between the lining of the shell and the dome in a sort of blister. When pearlers see a lump on the inside of a pearl shell they always break it open, for this reason. Many species of mollusks share the Oyster's ability to protect itself by coating irritants with lining material, but if their lining material is not pearly, a gem pearl will not be found in them. Clams, for example, form heavy, opaque, white beads that look like the china-white lining of their shells. Some Univalves with nacreous linings are able to make valuable pearls; one sea captain tells of finding a pearl he later sold for $50 in a large Conch taken from the Caribbean.

The value of a pearl depends on its lustre, or *orient*, as well as on its shape. Orient is caused by microscopic ripples in the thin layers of semi-transparent nacre that make up a pearl; when light strikes the ripples they act as prisms, breaking the light up into the spectrum and giving the pearl the soft iridescence that we consider beautiful. The degree of translucence and freedom from flaws determine the quality of the orient. Value is also affected by color; pearls may be white, yellowish, pink, green, brown, blue, or even black. Black and pink pearls are rare, and are prized for their beauty; white pearls are always in demand; but very few women want a necklace of green or brown pearls, and so these have little commercial value. Many pearls that are outwardly perfect have flaws in inner layers. A flawed outer layer of an otherwise fine pearl can be removed by a skilled jeweler to show the perfect layers hidden within.

The finest natural pearls come from the Pacific. They are made by mollusks more closely related to Mussels than to Oysters, but we call them Pearl Oysters. The shells are characterized by silvery-gold or black rims; they are worth $4 or $5 each. The "gold lip" is large, 12 inches across, and weighs as much as 10 pounds at maturity. The "black lip," which produces most of the pearls, is smaller and has little commercial value. While pearls offer a chance of sudden wealth, it is shell that feeds the diver and his family.

In the old days most of the divers were island men, who went down from canoes carrying weights to help them sink rapidly. Pearl shell is found covered with barnacles and weed; a worker without an artificial air supply would scarcely have time to find one shell and pry it loose before he had to come up for air. Shell accumulated slowly by this method. Later the old-fashioned diving suit, with helmet and weighted corselet, came into use. The diver walked along the bottom beneath his pearling boat (called a "lugger"), but he was often tugged off balance by currents pulling at his lifeline and air hose. Even with three or four men working the sea bed from each lugger the method was risky and inefficient.

Pearl diving has always been a dangerous business. The killers that make headlines are sharks, manta rays, and poisonous sea snakes; but most fatal accidents are caused by the deep-sea paralysis that strikes without warning when a diver breathes highly compressed air for long periods, until the lungs and bloodstream become saturated with it, or by what are called the "bends." The name describes the contorted body of a diver who is brought to the surface too quickly to allow the nitrogen bubbles that formed in his blood under pressure of the water above him to dissolve.

Some of the finest pearls the world has ever seen are gathered in the waters of the Torres Strait, between New Guinea and northern Australia. On Darnley Island, near this strait, is a cemetery which is the last resting place of many a diver. In the famous Darnley Deeps, shell is abundant, enticing the unwary and the greedy to stay down too long; forty fathoms of water and a sea bed which is a mountain range in miniature are a murderous combination. Local pearlers call the area the Divers' Graveyard.

The warm coastal waters off India provide an ideal habitat for pearl shell, and also for sharks. Indian divers go through a curious rite before entering the water: they are blessed by "shark charmers," who accompany them in the boats for this purpose.

Pearls are gathered from nacre-lined Mussels and fresh-water Clams, too; but these mollusks are principally harvested for their shells, which are made into mother-of-pearl buttons. Fresh-water pearls are beautiful; they have a greater iridescence and sheen than most salt-water pearls, though they lack the delicate, muted glow and softened lustre of the latter. Fresh-water pearls are usually baroque, and make attractive and interesting necklaces.

Mother-of-pearl buttons are still turned out in enormous numbers, though many substitute materials are now available. The great Pearl Oysters of the Pacific are the source of prime buttons; Thursday Island, off the coast of Australia, mushroomed to wealth overnight as a center for the industry. Just before the first world war, however, someone found that the common, shallow-water Trochus shell made good buttons. The underside of a button made of Trochus shell is not quite smooth, showing streaks of the brown, green, or red outer layer, and after a number of washings the button may turn yellow. Genuine pearl shell buttons retain their whiteness and are white all through, for the Pearl Oyster has an extremely thick lining of nacre. Now, however, an even cheaper substitute than Trochus has appeared: plastic. Man-made pearl buttons have replaced the genuine article on all mass-produced clothing, giving the coup-de-grace to the pearl shell industry.

Like other creatures, Oysters suffer from parasites. Tiny crabs, and a species of small fish, like to hide in their mantles. The female pea crab, a round little parasite about half an inch long, lives on the gills of the Bivalve, eating the food particles her host strains from the water. Her mate occasionally visits her, but apparently prefers the dangers of the outside world to her cloistered existence. If these parasites die and irritate the mollusk they are embalmed in mother-of-pearl tombs. Centuries ago some observant Oriental found one of these pearly tombs, and put his knowledge to use; the Chinese built a flourishing business on the sale of tiny, pearl-coated images of Buddha! They placed the porcelain or metal figures in Oysters or Mussels and left them for a year or so, until they were well coated with nacre. Images made this way are sold today in many parts of Asia.

Before long a Japanese man named Mikimoto tried putting a little round bead in an Oyster to see if pearls could be made in the same way. A long series of experiments produced the first cultured pearl; production of these man-assisted pearls is now a major industry in Japan and the Mediterranean. Thousands of people are employed on Japanese pearl farms, where they collect young Oysters, rear them in underwater cages, inject them with tiny beads of special shell material, and tend them for years until finally they can harvest a crop of cultured pearls.

A fine cultured pearl looks exactly like a genuine pearl. Cultured pearls do not always turn out as perfect spheres, and a great deal of effort and attention goes into their production, so they are fairly expensive. A single string of off-white cultured pearls of poor orient can be bought quite cheaply, but a strand of perfectly matched or graduated milk-white, iridescent beauties is expensive.

The lovely jewelry which is made from the mother-of-pearl lining of the Abalone has already been mentioned. Many women wear another piece of shell jewelry without realizing its origin: the cameo. Long ago a craftsman whittled a Conch from the warm waters off North Africa, and found that its white or cream exterior layer on a darker base could be carved into delicate bas-reliefs. Thus an industry was born. The Conchs, of the Cassia family, are often called Helmet Shells; they are exported to southern Italy, where skilled artisans cut them into discs and ovals and master craftsmen carve the delicate scenes. Cameos were highly fashionable in the Victorian era, when huge brooches and rings were popular. In Europe, cameos are still popular, but the jewelry produced today is small and delicate, in modern fashion.

There are few women who can resist the appeal of a fine pearl necklace or fail to admire a cameo ring; there are few people of either sex or any age who can see a collection of exquisite shells without feelings of wonder and awe. Delicate colors and fanciful shapes combine in infinite variety to captivate the beholder. If you have the opportunity to see the outstanding collection of the Shell Museum at Fort Myers, Florida, you will stay longer than you ever intended, held rooted before cases of red and pink and lavender Thorny Oysters, of snow-white fragile cradles of the Chambered Nautilus, of mauve-purple Janthinas and multi-colored Jewel-Box Shells, of pearl-lined Abalones and rose-valved Tellins. Fashions in jewelry come and go, but so long as people respond to beauty, seashells will be collected and cherished; for now, as in the past and future, the shells on our beaches are truly jewels of the sea displayed free for the taking.

Happy shelling!

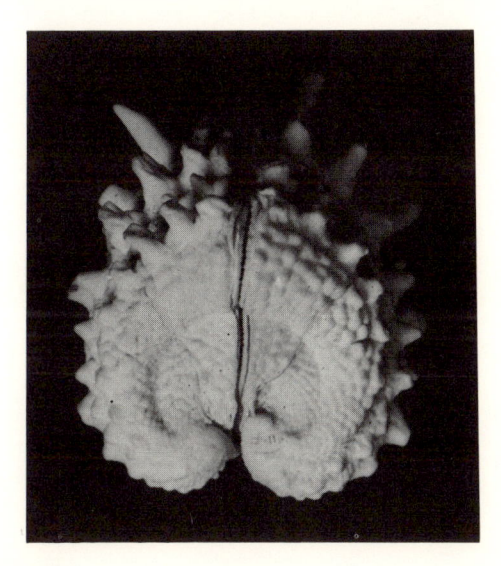

FLORIDA SPINY JEWEL BOX
Arcinella cornuta—1½″
The Spiny Jewel Box spends its life attached to a small bit of shell or rock. When the attachment breaks and the shell is finally washed up on the beach, you can find the scar close to the beak of the right valve.

Index

Abalones, 39, 47, 61, 88, 89, 92, 93
abyssal, 7
acid, effect on shells, 47, 69
acid, of predators, 30, 33
adductor muscles, 10, 11, 31, 32
age of shell life, 15, 29, 39
air bladders, 37
Alaska, 78
albino Conchs, 52, 59
alcohol, as preservative, 68
alcohol, in cleaning, 66
Algarve, Portugal, 65
Alpine mountains, 66
Alps, 74
American Indians, 79, 82
Amphineura, 12, 38, 46
"anchors," 13, 19, 22, 36, 61
Angel Wings, 44, 45
ants, as cleaners, 67
aperture, 8, 9
apex, 11
appearance, classing by, 15
Apple Murex, 58
archeologists, 73
Arks, 30, 65, 69, 70
arm, Cephalopod, 25
armlets, shell, 82
Arthritic Spider Conch, 24
assassins, 29
Atlantic Moon Snail, 22
Atlantic Slipper Shell, 42
Atlantic Winged Oyster, 61
Australia, 65, 91
axis, 7
Aztecs, 80, 81

bag, for shells, 41
Banded Snails, 66
Banded Tulip, 59
bar, for collecting, 41
barnacles, 35, 47, 67
baroque pearl, 90
Bat Volute, 53
beachworn shells, 5
beak, Octopus, 17, 39
beauty, value of, 75
"bends," 91
Bering Strait, 78
Bible, 74
Bishop's Miter 59
Bivalves, 10, 11, 21, 25, 66
"black lip" shells, 90
Bleeding Tooth Nerite, 50
Blue-Rayed Limpet, 49
body plan, classing by, 15
body whorl, 8, 9
boiling, 67, 68
boxes, 41, 72
Brachiopods, ancient, 65
brain, Octopus, 14
Brown Paper Argonaut, 13
Buccinum Whelk, 22
bucket, for collecting, 41
Buddha, 92
Buttercup Lucina, 63
butterfly boxes, 72
buying shells, 70
byssus, 19, 61, 78

cabinet, metal storage, 72
calcium carbonate, 27
Calico Clam, 63
Calico Scallop, 62
California laws, 39, 47
cameos, 26, 57, 92
camouflage, 16, 19, 20, 22, 23, 26, 36, 46, 49, 64
camp stove, 68
cannibals, 29, 30, 34, 35
Caribbean, 90
carnivores, 29, 36, 59, 60
carotenoid pigment, 26
Carrier Shell, 39
"cat's eyes," 59, 85
Cephalopoda, 13, 14, 19, 25, 38, 60
ceremonial mask, 81
chain of food, 29
Chambered Nautilus, 60, 93
Channeled Duck Clam, 30
Checkerboard Clam, 63
Cherrystones, 88
China, 88
Chinese Alphabet Cone, 60
Chitons, 12, 21, 41, 46, 68
chowder, 88, 89
chromatophores, 20
chondrophore, 30
cilia, 21, 38
Clam, Channeled Duck, 30
Clam chowder, 88
Clam, defenses of, 33
Clam digging, 45
Clam eggs, 21
Clam, fossil, 65, 73
Clam, Giant, 4, 83, 84
Clam, Hard Shell, 46, 88
Clam kabobs, 81
Clam, life span of, 39
Clam, Lima, 31
Clam, movement of, 31
Clam, Razor, 31
Clam, Royal Comb Venus, 30
Clams, 4, 23, 36, 40, 63, 79, 90, 91
Clams, smoked, 81
classes, evolution of, 15
classes, mollusk, 7
cleaning shells, 66
Clearwater, Florida, 65
cliffs, danger of, 46
"cloth of gold," 78
Coat-of-Mail shells, 12, 78
Cockle, Eggshell, 96
Cockles, 3, 63, 88, 96
coil, Nautilus, 15
collecting, 41
collection building, 70
colonies, 42, 58
color, 12, 19, 20, 35, 48, 62
colors, fading, 5, 48
columella, 7, 45
Conch, Arthritic Spider, 24
Conch, Drilling, 19
Conch eggs, 21
Conch, Florida Crown, 26
Conch, Florida Fighting, 52
Conch, Giant, 9
conchiolin, 24, 25, 35
Conch, life span of, 39
Conch, Orange Spider, 52
Conchs, 7, 27, 33, 37, 43, 45, 53, 79, 90, 92
Cone Shells, 37, 60, 69, 70, 85, 86
Conquistadors, 81
Coon Oysters, 45
Coquina Clams, 88
Coquinas, 45, 69, 87
coral deposits, 69
coral reefs, 4, 47
cornea, Octopus, 14
Cortez, Hernando, 81
cosmetics, from Murex, 77
Costa del Sol, Spain, 65
cotton, for collecting, 41
cotton, for display, 71
country of origin, 70
Cowries, 26, 27, 54, 60, 67, 70, 85, 86
crabs, 39
cradle, egg, 14, 19
crochet hook, in cleaning, 66, 68
Cro-Magnon Man, 73
Cross-Barred Venus, 40
Cross-Hatched Lucine, 96
Crown Conch, 26
Crusades, 77
crystals, shell, 27
"cultching" oyster beds, 87
Cuttlefish, 15, 39

dangers in collecting, 46
dangers to Bivalves, 31-37
dangers to Snails, 35
Darnley Deep, 91
dead shells, 40
decay of shellfish, 66
Deltoid Rock Shell, 51
Dentalium, 79
deposit feeders, 31
dextral shells, 7
displaying shells, 66, 69
Divers' Graveyard, 91
Dog Whelks, 35
Dog Winkle, 22
Dosinia, Elegant, 34
dredging for shells, 46
drifts, shell, 65
drill holes, 30
Drilling Conchs, 19, 88
ducts, Cone, 37
duplicate specimens, 71
dye, first, 59
Dye, Murex, 76
dyes from shells, 59, 76, 79

earplugs, shell, 82
Ear Shells, 47
East Coast Clam, 88
eelgrass, 38
egg cases, 22, 23
egg cradles, 13, 14, 19
egg float, 17
eggs, fertilization of, 21
Egg Shell Cockle, 96
Egg Shells, 56
Elegant Dosinia, 34
Elephant Tooth Shell, 12
Emerald Nerite, 51
epidermis, 27, 69
Escargots, 89
Euphrates, 75
European Cowries, 54
European Oyster beds, 87
evolution of mollusks, 16, 24
Eyed Cowrie, 26
eyes, Gastropoda, 7
eyes, Octopus, 14

face mask, 43
False Angel Wing, 44
false lips, counting, 29
families, collecting, 70
farming, Mussel, 88
farming, Oyster, 38, 87, 88
feeding, 13, 31
fertilization, 21
Fig Shell, 50
Fiji, Crown Jewel Shell, 85
fins, 18

94

first shells, 15
floating Snails, 17
Florida Cerith, 4
Florida Crown Conch, 26
Florida Fighting Conch, 52
Florida Horn Shell, 4
Florida Keys, 42, 44, 65
Florida Queen Conchs, 37
Florida Spiny Jewel Box, 93
Florida Thorny Oyster, 63
Florida Tree Snail, 51
Florida, sponge diving in, 48
food, chain of, 29
food, for gulls, 33, 38
food, for whales, 10, 39
food, of mollusks, 25, 33, 38, 45
food, shells as, 4, 6, 74, 87-89
food supply, sea, 21
foot, 7, 13, 21, 28, 36
formation of shells, 25
Fort Myers Museum, 93
fossils, 16, 65, 70, 73
frail shells, handling, 68
France, 89
freshly dead shells, 5
Frilled Venus, 64
Furbelow Clam, 4

Garden Snail, 6, 66
Gastropoda, 7, 8, 35
gear, for collecting, 41
Geography Cone, 86
geologists, 6
Giant Clams, 4, 83, 84
Giant Conchs, 9
Giant Tun, 50
gills, 9, 17
girdle, 69
Glorious Scallop, 62
Glory of the Seas Cone, 37, 86
Golden Cowrie, 85
"gold lip" shells, 90
"grapes," 25
Greece, sponge diving in, 48
Green Star Shell, 49
Green Turban, 28
grouping specimens, 70
gulls, 33, 38

habitats, 23
handling frail shells, 68
Hard Shell Clams, 46, 88
Harp Shell, 54
"hatchet-foot," 10
Hawk-Wing Conch, 24
"head-footed," 14
Heart Cockle, 3
Helmet Shells, 26, 57, 92
herbivores, 29, 59
hermit crab, 43
hinge, 10, 11, 30, 32
holdfasts, 38
homesites, 38
Hooked Mussel, 61
horns, 7
Horn Shell, Florida, 4
Hump Back Cowrie, 55
hunting for shells, 5

Ice Age, 78
Ice Age, bones from, 79
identification, 71
identification guide, 6, 70
Incas, 81
index card file, 71
Indian Ocean Cowries, 74
Indonesians, 84
ink, Cuttlefish, 39

ink, Murex, 76
ink, Squid, 39
inner layer, of shell, 27
invertebrates, 7
iridescence, pearl, 90, 92
Italy, 74

jade green shell, 12
Janthinas, 17, 56, 65, 93
Japan, 65, 88, 89
Jason's Golden Fleece, 78
Java Man, 78
jellyfish, 19
Jerusalem, 77
Jewel Box Shell, 93
jewelry making, 89-93

kelp, 38, 45
Key Vaca, Florida, 65
Key West, Florida, 65
King Helmet, 57
Kitchen-Midden People, 74, 81
kitchen middens, 38

labelling specimens, 71
Lace Murex, 36
Laciniated Conch, 24
Lamellose Wentletrap, 52
Land Slugs, 9
Land Snails, 17, 66, 70, 89
larvae, 21, 25
Latin names, 71
laundry bleach, 69
layers, shell, 27
Left-handed Whelk, 58
legal protection of shells, 66, 87
legend of Giant Clam, 84
Lettered Olive, 58
Lettered Venus, 64
Leucodon Cowrie, 86
Lightning Whelk, 22, 58
Lima Clams, 31
lime deposits, 69
Limpet, Blue-Rayed, 49
Limpet, Lister's Keyhole, 18
Limpets, 17, 18, 19, 37, 38, 49
Limpets, deceiving, 38
Limpet, Striped False, 49
lining, shell, 27
Lion's Paw, 62
lip, 8, 9, 24, 27, 36, 68, 90
lips, false, 29
Lister's Keyhole Limpet, 18
Lister's Tree Oyster, 20
Little Neck Clams, 88
littoral, 7
living mollusks, 39
lobsters, 39
local names, 71
Lucine, Pennsylvania, 34
Lucine, Tiger, 34, 96
luggers, pearl, 91
lungs, 17
Lynx Cowrie, 54

magnifying glass, 65
mantle, 9, 10, 26, 27, 84, 89
mantle's edge, 27
mantle tissue, 27, 89
margins, 11, 34
Marlinspike, 60
mask, Aztec, 80, 81
Matanavat, 82
Mediterranean, 74, 89
Mediterranean Murex, 75
melanin pigment, 26
Mexico, 77, 80, 81
middens, 74
Middle Ages, shells in, 77

middle layer, of shell, 27
Midget Harp, 54
Mikimoto, 92
milting, 21
mineral oil, 69
miniature shells, 65
Minnesota Minnie, 78
Miters, 59
Mollusca, phylum, 7
mollusks, classes of, 7
Money Cowrie, 54
money, shell, 54, 79, 82, 83, 85
Montezuma, 81
Moon Snail, 22, 23, 29, 33, 43
mosaics, shell, 80, 81, 82
Moses, 77
mother-of-pearl, 75, 85, 86, 87, 88, 91
Murex, 36, 37, 58, 75, 76
muscles, 10
museum collections, 70
Mussels, 19, 35, 61, 87, 88, 91, 92
mutations, 16
Mutton Fish, 47
Mycenae, 66

nacre, 60, 89
Naples, Italy, 89
Nassas, 35
natural selection, 16
Nautilus, 14
necklaces, seashell, 73, 82, 83, 85
"necks," 31
Nerite, Bleeding Tooth, 50
Nerite, Emerald, 51
Nerites, 45, 50, 51
New Guinea, 85, 91
New Hebrides, 82
nightfeeders, 58
nocturnal Snails, 66
notebook, specimen, 71
nuclear whorl, 8, 9
Nudibranchs, 9, 48
numbering shells, 71
Nutmeg Shell, 59

Octopus, 14, 17, 19, 25, 38, 39, 89
oil deposits, 6
Old Testament, 74, 77
Olive Nerite, 50
Olive Shells, 45, 67
opercula, 8, 9, 28, 29, 67, 85
Orange Spider Conch, 52
orient, of pearls, 90, 92
orifices, feeding, 31
Ormers, 47
ornaments, shells as, 6, 73, 82, 89
overcollection, 39, 44, 47, 87
Oyster cultivation, 88
Oyster Drills, 33
Oyster farmers, 38, 87
oyster, life span of, 39
Oyster, Pearl, 90, 91
Oysters, 20, 21, 23, 36, 37, 38, 39, 61, 63, 87-88
Oyster shell roads, 87
Oysters, protection of, 33
Oysters, Thorny, 32, 37, 63

pair shell, 10
pallial line, 10, 11
pallial sinus, 10, 11
Papal Miter, 59
Paper Argonaut, 14
parasites, 92
parasitic larvae, 25
pea crab, 92
pearl diving, 91
pearl, first cultured, 92

95

pearling boat, 91
Pearl Oysters, 90, 91
pearls, 89, 90, 91
pearl shell, 91
Pearly Nautilus, 60, 93
Peking Man, 78
pelagic, 7, 19
Pelecypoda, 10
pen, for marking, 71
Pennsylvania Lucine, 34
perfect specimens, 40, 41
periostracum, 44, 69
Periwinkles, 37-38, 46, 89
Periwinkle, Zigzag, 51
Peru, 81
Philippine Islands, 65, 86
Phoenicians, 75
photosynthesis, 37
phylum Mollusca, 7
Piddocks, 31
pinch bar, 41
Pink-mouthed Murex, 58
Pinnas, 78
plankton, 21
Pliny the Elder, 89
poison, Cone Shell, 37
poisonous darts, 10
Polynesians, 84
population, shell, 6
Portugal, 65
pottery, shell-inlaid, 79
predators, 26, 30, 34, 59
prehistoric shells, 73
preserving mollusk bodies, 68
Prickly Paper Cockle, 63
protection of shells, 66, 87
Pteropods, 10
Purple, 22
purple ink of Murex, 75
Purple Sea Snail, 56

Quahogs, 79, 88

radar protection, 87
radula, Limpet, 17
radula, of Snail, 30, 33
raft, Janthina, 17
Ramose Murex, 58
Razor Clam, 31
Red Abalone, 61
Red Sea Cowries, 74
repairing shells, 29
reptiles, 15
Reticulated Cowrie, 55
retina, Octopus, 14
revival of Periwinkles, 46
ridged shells, 19, 27, 40
roads, of Oyster shells, 87
rock dwellers, 46
rock shelters, disturbing, 46
Rose Petal Tellin, 64
Rose Tellins, 65
Round Clams, 88
Royal Comb Venus Clam, 30
royal purple, 77

St. Petersburg, Florida, 65
Sand Dollars, 43
Sanibel Island, Florida, 65, 78
Scallops, 31, 47, 62, 77, 87
Scandinavia, 78
Scaphopoda, 12, 38
scars, 11, 29, 93
scavengers, 4, 26, 29, 43
scientists, 6, 71
"scrub balls," 22
sculptured shells, 44, 96
sea anemones, 10, 48

Sea Butterflies, 10, 18
sea grasses, 45
Sea Hares, 9
Sea Slugs, 9
Sea Snails, floating, 17
seaweed, 37, 46
sepia pigment, 39
septa, 15
sex changes, 42, 87
shape, of Univalves, 25
sheen and color, 5
shell catalogue, 71
shelling from boats, 48
Shell Museum, Florida, 93
shell pearls, 90
shells, hunting for, 5
shells, sheen and color, 5
Shipworms, 31
shoes, on reefs, 48
Short-spined Star Shell, 44
shovel, for collecting, 41
Shuttle Shell, 40
Siberia, 78
Silver Lip Conch, 53
sinistral shells, 9
siphonal notch, 8
siphons, 23, 34
skindiving, 47, 48
Slipper Shell, 42, 71, 88
Slugs, 7, 9
Smithsonian Institution, 71
smooth shells, 27
Snail dye, 75
Snail, Florida Tree, 51
Snail, Green Turban, 28
Snail, Moon, 22, 23, 29, 33, 43
Snails, 7, 16, 23, 28, 35, 45, 56, 59, 68, 89
Snails, cannibalistic, 30, 34, 35
Snails, fossil, 70
snails, movement of, 28
Snails, Land, 17
Snails, nocturnal, 66
Snipe's Bill Murex, 36
soft-bodied animals, 7
Solomon Islands, 83, 85
South America, 78
Spain, 65, 88
"spat," 87
spawning, 83
species, collecting, 70
species, number of, 6
spermatozoa, 25
spiked shells, 27
Spiny Paper Cockle, 63
spiraled shells, cleaning, 68
spine, 8, 9
Spirula, 13, 14
"spoiling out," 67
Spondylus, 85
Squid, 13, 14, 19, 25, 39, 89
Starfish, 33
Star Shells, 44, 45, 49
Stone Age, 74
storage units, 71, 72
storms, effect on shells, 65
Striped Bonnet, 53
Striped False Limpet, 49
suction disc, 17
Sulu Archipelago, 4
Sumerians, 74
sunburn, danger of, 48
Sundial Shell, 56
Sunray Venus, 64
suspension feeders, 31
symmetry, bilateral, 25
Syria, 77

Tapestry Turban, 59
teeth, 10, 11, 30, 32
teeth, of Oyster drills, 33
Tehauntepec Indians, 77
Tellins, 35, 64, 65, 70, 93
temperature, effect on mollusks, 29, 67
Tent Cone, 60
Ten Thousand Islands, Florida, 65
Teredo infestations, protection from, 33
Teredos, 31, 43
Tessellate Nerite, 50
Texas Tusk Shell, 13
Textile Cone, 60
Thais shells, 68
thickness, shell, 12, 27
Thorny Oysters, 32, 37, 63, 93
3-ply shells, 27
Thursday Island, 91
tidepools, 43
tide-tables, 43, 47
Tiger Cowrie, 55
Tiger Lucine, 34, 96
tongue depressors, 41, 46
Torres Strait, 91
trading, shells, 66, 70, 88
translucence, pearl, 90
trapdoor, 9
trays, for display, 71
Triton's Trumpet, 57
trochophores, 21, 25
Trochus shell, 91
True Tulip, 59
trumpets, shell, 57
Tulip Shells, 59
Tun, Giant, 50
Turban Snails, 85
Turkey Wing, 61
Turret Shell, 52
Tusk Shell, 12, 13, 65, 79
tweezers, in cleaning, 66, 67
Tyre, 75, 76
Tyrian coins, 77
Tyrian purple, 75, 76

umbones, 10, 11
Univalves, 9, 25, 67, 70
Ur, 74
uses of shells, 6, 23, 57
utensils, shells as, 6, 57

value, in ancient times, 75
valves, 10, 11, 62
varices, 8, 29
vegetarians, 38
veligers, 21
Venus clams, 30, 40, 64
Vikings, 78

wampum, 79
weather, factor in shelling, 65
Wentletrap, 52
West Indian Bubble, 51
West Indian Worm Shell, 42
Whelks, 23, 35, 58, 89
"whiskers," Ark, 69
whorls, 8, 9, 60
Winged Oysters, 65
wing-footed, 10
Worm Shell, West Indian, 40
wrack, 38

Yellow Tellins, 65

Zigzag Periwinkle, 51
Zigzag Scallop, 62

96